Listen to what your colleagues are saying

"Power Calling is one of those "magic keys" professionals look for. It works." — Joseph Charbonneau, motivational speaker.

"I found Joan Guiducci's approach creative and new. It's a winner." —Jack Hymes, real estate agent.

"My business soared more than 30% in about three months by reading Power Calling a little every day."—Gene Powers, computer product sales.

"This book creates order out of prospecting chaos." —Christopher J. Derry, president of a marketing technologies company.

"Power Calling is an excellent and practical book." —Jeff Wrench, insurance agent.

"I feel confident and relaxed about making cold calls." —Suzanne Ishimaru, interior designer.

"Of all the how-to books I've read, this has the most examples." —Rita Behymer, consultant.

"I'd recommend this book to any old pro and it's a must for all the rookies."—Mark Allen, printing company representative.

"I found Power Calling easy to use and the advice so very clear." —David Christian, auctioneer.

"Plunk down your $14.95. It's worth it."—Joan Guiducci, author.

JOAN GUIDUCCI'S
POWER CALLING®

A Fresh
Approach To
Cold Calls
& Prospecting

Power Calling®
A Fresh Approach to Cold Calls & Prospecting
Copyright © 1992, Joan Guiducci.
Power Calling is a registered trademark of Tonino.
All rights reserved.

Editorial director
Kristen Muller Levine

Graphics
Hazel Design of San Francisco

ISBN 1–881833–00–3

Printed in the United States of America.

In memory of my Aunt Ruth

When you cannot see what is
happening, do not stare
harder. Relax and look gently
with your inner eye.

—**John Heider**
The Tao of Leadership

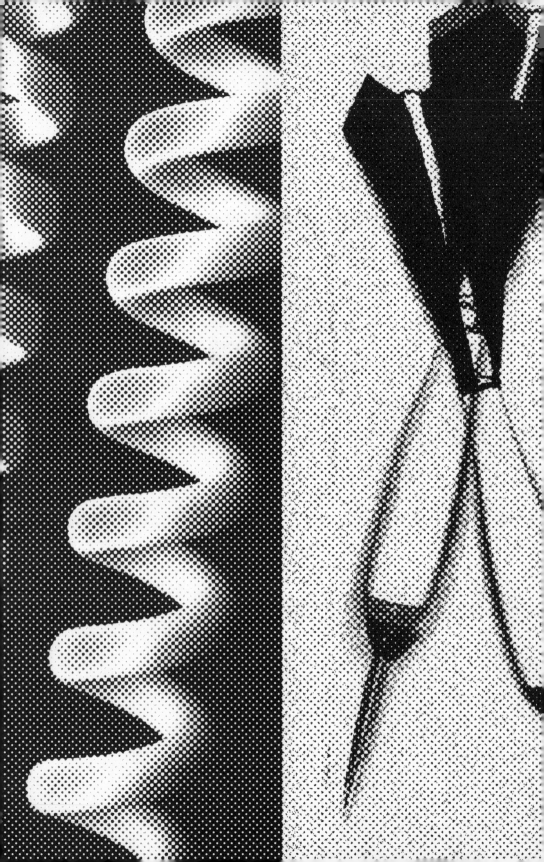

Table of Contents

Acknowledgements   To my husband, Gino, who was always there. And to my editor, Kristen, who has an extrordinary vision for the written word and with whom I had the joy of collaborating. Much thanks to my designer, Amy, for making Power Calling look great. My sincere and deepest appreciation goes to Craig and Julie Beck, Dan Byrne, Phyllis Warton and the family for their encouragement and suggestions. Thanks to you all.

Joan Guiducci

Introduction

Cold calling without results is a drag on your business, and on you. When you hang up the telephone feeling dissatisfied, worn-out and defeated, it's no wonder you harbor such resistance toward each minute, hour, and day of cold calling. This book will ease the pain.

Mostly, those first calls fail because you are not prepared—you don't know what to say. Well, if you follow this step-by-step approach, you'll be comfortable (and successful!) with every cold call.

This book shows you how to deliver a powerful message that will catch people's curiosity. Prospects will sit up and listen. If you know who you are and use the power you have—prospects will want to hear what you have to say. They will begin to trust you and want to do business with you. Prospects will become loyal clients and you'll make more money.

Imagine dialing each number with a fresh attitude, as though it were the first call of the day, not the tenth or twentieth.

And it's time you recognize the telephone as a powerful, and positive vehicle for marketing your wares and qualifying your leads.

I have developed my methods for getting past the grumble through my own trial and error. I'm a 20 year veteran of telephone prospecting, and don't subscribe to the tired and tried hard-sell method. Why? It's too difficult. And it makes the telephone gain about 20 pounds.

The effective first call travels beyond simply announcing new products or services. In this book, I show you how "drawing" pictures of your prospects makes it easier to find them. When you do, you'll tell your "story," making optimum use of your time by developing vital—not idle—conversation.

In the following chapters, you'll encounter examples of sample dialogue. Read these aloud. On paper, they may not sound so natural, but when spoken, these words become real dialogue. Avoid sounding scripted—a sure hang-up for prospects. Use these dialogues as spurs to your own creativity and imagination. Just be yourself and be persistent. Use your own language and choose vocabulary that feels comfortable. If you're not sure how you sound, record your side of the conversation and smooth your quirks. Soon, you'll experience profitable telephone calls.

I don't believe in rejection. Sure, you'll run into a few people that are unwilling to listen to you, to hear new ideas. Through my years of prospecting I can honestly count and remember those conversations—and there haven't been many. It is true, however, that the process of refining your cold-calling skills and staying with your product or service can be challenging. Sometimes you call a lot of people before you reach the one who needs what you are selling, now. But the more numbers you dial, the more prospects you'll qualify.

Take good notes and set aside time—daily or weekly—for telephone prospecting. You'll find this book so helpful, you'll keep reaching for it when your skills grow a little rusty.

In the meantime, reach into the heart of sales—your belief in your business and yourself. Remember, each cold call is the first step toward building a new business relationship. Make it your rule to apply

integrity, honesty, and directness in making these calls—because selling without hype is what works these days.

> —Joan Guiducci

CHAPTER 1

1
Prospects— who and where are they?

Play darts, win big

So here you are planning to expand your business through telephone prospecting. Let me tell you, if you don't devise a strategy for cold calling, you're bound to waste a lot of time.

Naturally, you can't just pick up the white pages and telephone all the "l's" this morning and the "m's" this afternoon. People who don't have carpets will not purchase one hundred cases of your carpet cleaner. They won't even buy one tube. Your goal is to contact the right people, the people who need your service or product. Let's begin now, to color in a picture of our prospect—that person or business whom we suspect has a need for what we're selling.

So, who is your prime prospect? In a sense, I see telephone prospecting is like playing a game of darts. The center circle represents my ideal client. If we continually aim for the bulls-eye, we'll reach our targeted buyer groups. If we randomly toss the darts, we'll hit the wall.

On your dart board, each concentric circle may represent a geographic or demographic boundary, or both. To create a profile of your ideal prospect, ask yourself plenty of questions. What does my prospect look like? How does she make a living? What does he do for fun? Where does she live? Am I selling primarily to a business? What size business? What industry? Which departments of what companies? Am I selling to home-owners? In what income bracket? Am I trying to reach certain neighborhoods or specific age groups? Do I want to find the baby-boomers' babies now living in the Western United States, including Hawaii? Or just the elderly in my hometown?

The more clearly you define your prospect, the more likely you are to hit the bulls-eye. For example, if I see my prospects as 5'7" brunettes with brown eyes, 90 percent of whom wear contact lenses, then the blue tinted contact lenses I'm marketing are bound to appeal to many of them (who hasn't wanted to change eye color?), and the more success I am going to enjoy. You'll soon notice how niches can be wide and shallow or very narrow, yet deep. Once you have determined boundaries, got that clear-cut, ideal prospect defined, it only makes sense that finding your prospects is going to be much, much easier.

Power Calling begins

Twenty-plus years of cold calling had made an expert out of me. I was making a great living prospecting other people's products. My schedule was busy conducting cold-caller

What size business?
Which departments of what companies?
To what income bracket?
Am I selling to homeowners?
Am I selling to what income bracket?
What industry?
geographic boundaries?
Are there geographic boundaries?
DEMOGRAPHIC
Where do they buy?

training programs within companies. I was also finally getting serious about developing this book, but knew I needed help. I had to find a writer, and fast, to smooth out the rough edges in my writing and to help me organize my ideas in book form.

And once I'd decided to get serious about developing my cold-calling expertise into a book, I "happened" on a card that read "Kristen Muller writer • editor" on a bulletin board at the neighborhood grocery store. I contacted Kristen, engaged in a productive conversation, and needless to say, she and I have ended up writing *Power Calling*. She was prospecting to entrepreneurs. Her potential clients were small businesses in close proximity. And I happened to be the bulls-eye on her dart board.

Observe the obvious

As the writing of this book came to a close, Kristen mentioned having to begin looking for more clients. "Do you read your junk mail?" I asked her. She thought I was joking. "Well, you should," I said.

It's true, businesses must watch how others reach prospective buyers, but there's more. The very people who are trying to solicit your business, may be prospects for your own goods or services.

I knew a designer who studied all that paper clutter stuffed in her mailbox: catalogues, advertisements, direct mailers, and newsletters. Weekly, she'd learn where these advertisers were located, and she'd cold call these companies, introduce herself, and then probe. She'd say, "I have some fresh design ideas for you. I am confident I can make your direct mail more effective. How are you producing your newsletters? . . . I think we should meet." Very few people said "no" to her; they had nothing to lose and plenty to gain.

Like I said, look around you. Your prospects exist down the street, across the boulevard, in every town.

Suppose you own a signage company. While running your own errands, you see several stores that could use your help. Here's a suggestion. Call them. After you introduce yourself say, "I was in your store yesterday. You've done a great job remodeling the interior. What are your plans for the outside? . . . I know some exterior changes would increase foot traffic. I nearly passed by your shop, so that means others must, too. I'll be downtown tomorrow. I'd like to drop by and show you some of my ideas for your business."

Observe the obvious sources in the directory listing the businesses in office buildings, or while driving to and from appointments. In fact, if you're successful in a specific part of town, why not call on other nearby businesses?

"I'm in your part of town every week visiting my clients, I'd like to stop in and introduce myself." But before you make these calls, talk to those local clients for any inside information they may have on these potential prospects. Perhaps they'll even serve as a reference for you.

By the way, we all know the frustration of being blessed with a great idea, and then forgetting it just as quickly. Always carry a tape recorder or a notebook with you to capture every new plan, and follow through, or don't. Not every idea pans out.

Network for more work

TIPSTER
Call your clients
and ask for
ideas and
new contact names.

Consider what other businesses share prospect profiles similar to the one you've developed. If you are a seamstress, offer bridal shops your alteration expertise. A landscaper might drive through neighborhoods, looking for construction sites. Carpet cleaning services targeting affluent neighborhoods within a 10-mile radius might network with real estate agents and window washing services.

Pregnant women are natural prospects for diaper services, or maternity clothes. Call the obstetrician and ask her to help you prospect by allowing you to place flyers in her office, or to pin your card on her bulletin board. Physical therapy centers and healthclubs are prime sources for finding customers who will buy your high-tech bracelet that monitors heart rate and calorie consumption related to workouts.

I suggested Kristen and a graphic designer combine efforts. Separately they each have two leads and together they have four. Eventually, they might form their own networking group with printers, photographers, and so on.

Suppose you don't know anyone who might form a networking group with you. How do you find quality people with whom to associate? The solution is simple. Ask your clients for names of people they

Telephone Talk

trust. Then call those people and say, "We share a client. So-and-so has great respect for your work and mine, too. I thought we should talk. Perhaps we can pass some business on to each other."

And don't forget about local organized networking groups like the Chamber of Commerce. Check the local newspaper for a list of meetings scheduled that week. You may find local networking groups listed, too.

The list business builds big business

The telephone remains a valuable networking tool for screening out un-profitable prospects, making good use of time, and focusing your ener-gies on those most likely to buy your product or service. But sometimes you hit the wall. You've kept a clear picture of your prospect before you and yet perhaps you feel you've exhausted your narrow scope of con-tacts. Don't get discouraged, just concentrate on building your list of prospects. As you can imagine—and successful people will tell you—an up-to-date, well-maintained list is to be cherished. It's worth its length in gold.

Find out if a list of some sort already exists that would contain prospects for your product or service. Keep in mind, however, that we live in a fluid world and things change quickly. Families and businesses move and phone numbers are disconnected. Just be aware companies can be here and gone by the time extensive national directories get dis-tributed.

You might consider buying a list—it's a quick way of getting a lot of names. Some lists are very expensive, some are not. Likewise, some are easy to get; others not. List brokers are helpful if you can describe your ideal prospect to them.

Lists range from the broad to the specific. I've seen lists for American businesses using IBM mainframe computers, statewide radio talk show stations, and greenhouses in a county in northern Michigan. You may not be able to buy the names of all males 25 to 35 years old living west of the Mississippi who ride mountain bikes on sunny Sunday afternoons, but you may find the names of people over 50 who have had

TIPSTER

The very people who are trying to solicit your business may be prospects for your own wares.

plastic surgery in Miami.

Here's a warning about lists. They can be limited, and limiting if you get dependent on them. Several business in the same industry may be working from the same list, which means the same prospects are being cold called all day. Well, they won't want to hear from you after getting five similar calls. That's why you better be creative with your name gathering. Lists *you* build for *your* business over time have the most value.

Available for public consumption

You've networked. You've bought a list or two. How else do you build your prospecting list? Get familiar with the "mechanics" of your field—language, jargon, signals—that will help you anticipate changes in the economy and especially in companies or people that you perceive as prime prospects.

A travel agent I know scours every Sunday newspaper for engagement photos; she can arrange the perfect romantic honeymoon.

Learn to read all the business pages in your local newspaper. If you operate an outplacement service, contact corporations you suspect are planning a layoff.

Again, in the newspaper's business section, you'll find names of people promoted to new positions. For example, someone who sells healthclub memberships would use this information to call these movers and shakers (after waiting a few days for the dust to settle) and tout the benefits of stress reduction classes and regular workouts.

TIPSTER
Carry a tape recorder or a notebook to capture every new idea you have, and then follow through.

Be familiar with the classified sections, too. If I were a car mechanic, I'd call people in my neighborhood selling cars, and suggest they send buyers to me for the good deal on the required smog checks and registration inspections. If you run an event-planning business, look in the newspaper for companies doing well. They are possibly in a celebrating mood and may just be poised and "waiting" for your call. If I am an insurance agent I'd make a habit of reading personal announcements in the newspaper, such as births and marriages. New parents and newlyweds are getting serious about life and want to invest in their future.

Contact the staff on your city's business directory. The directory will show where to find record's of new licenses and building permits. Suppose you are an accounting firm servicing small companies. You'd want a monthly listing of all businesses issued a license, including those awarded in the last 2 years.

Your library's business section houses shelves of directories for specific industries and activities. I would start with the basics: <u>Standard and Poor's,</u> <u>Thomas Directory of Manufacturers,</u> <u>Dun and Bradstreet,</u> or the <u>Business Prospector.</u> Some references provide not only names and addresses of companies, but numbers of employees, names of controlling officers, and company assets.

Browse through the yellow pages, too. You may be surprised to find listings for categories you never knew existed. And talk to the librarian or members of the Chamber of Commerce. They usually have some suggestions. Don't forget your local telephone company; your representative might furnish you with a list of new business lines installed in recent months.

Reverse or criss-cross directories are backward telephone books, of sorts. Here you'll find listings arranged by street address followed by telephone number and name. This handy tool allows you to canvass specific neighborhoods. Remember human nature—most of us live with others like us, congregating by age, life-style, economic status, ethnic groupings.

Look to existing clients for prospects

Once when I was out of work, I thought, "What am I going to do?" My mind raced. Once I'd calmed down, I thought, "Why can't I work for myself?" I could market my skills and experience. Having settled that dilemma, I then asked myself, "Who am I going to call?" Ironically, in my question, I'd found the answer. I've been top producer selling office products, real estate, and software through cold calling at every firm where I'd been employed.

Well who were likely prospects? I knew the computer software community really well. Over time, I had developed an extensive mailing list, a benefit for any company who would hire me. I ran connections through my head. Aha! People can't use software without hardware. I

Telephone Talk

suspected hardware manufacturers were prime prospects, as well.

First, I checked my computer data base and dug out old address books. That led me to the telephone to talk with some long-time, familiar contacts. The two most productive questions I learned to ask were: Do you have any projects coming up that I may be able to help with? Do you know of anyone who needs my services? I made everyone aware of my plan. Before I knew it, I had plenty of clients.

Let's say you had been employed in advertising and you left the agency to start your own. You might try calling those clients you worked with before, unless there was a prohibitive clause in your contract. In any case, even if you can't ethically approach former clients as prospects, you can go to them and ask for help, or to use them as references. They may be flattered and contrary to what you may believe, they won't think you're imposing on them. Tell them what you're looking for. Ask for new contacts.

If former clients have confidence in your work, they'll want to help you out, to help you build new business relationships. And with new clients, keep in mind that in some respects a business relationship is like a friendship. When you find a loyal one, you'll want to nurture that connection. And remember too, who gave the names to you in the first place. Former or existing clients who help you deserve your loyalty and referrals.

TIPSTER
Behind each name on your list lives a human being.

Go where your clients go

If you're hunting for deer, don't wade through the duck pond. Try looking where you've spotted deer before. Your best prospect looks like someone who already buys your product or partakes in your service. Behind each name on your list lives a human being. Where do your loyal clientele go for goods and services? Your clients have friends, family, dentists, hair dressers, bankers. You get the idea. With charm and persistence, or a lunch date, you'll have club membership lists, company rosters, and local trade association membership rosters coming your way.

Heard it through the grapevine

I know a manicurist who used to live from paycheck to paycheck which is not unusual, many people do. But when the car needed repair and her daughter was planning a wedding, my manicurist had to increase her business. She called me and said, "Joan, I know how you love those pedicures, I'm having a special this month with every manicure."

"Great," I said, "I'll be there, but you've got to be a little bit more creative." I set the stage for her, gave her prospecting ideas, and one name led to another—sort of like a free-association game.

She suggested her clients bring a friend to the salon. This way, customers advertised for her without realizing it. Later, she hooked up with the tanning booth across the street. Then she began leaving piles of her business cards and brochures on the counter at health-clubs. She telephoned high school newspapers and ran an ad in the classified section offering a special deal for graduation, prom nights, Valentine's Day, New Years, you name it.

Referral prospecting is great fertilizer for your lists. And inexpensive too. I always subtly encourage customers and clients to prospect for me. Just ask for referrals: friends, neighbors, colleagues, church members. I find people have names at the tips of their tongues when you tickle their memories.

My sister lives in New England. Several autumns ago she painted a harvest scene on the windows of her friend's jewelry boutique. The elegant gourd and wheat image lured a number of buyers across the threshold. Other businesses on the mall came knocking, too. They suddenly needed their storefronts arranged for Halloween. My sister eventually developed something of a monopoly. Now she decorates businesses from Christmas to Thanksgiving and for every holiday between.

Oh, and never give just one business card to someone. Give each person three, that's what my sister does. This way when your client gives one or two away, he keeps one for himself. Word-of-mouth recommendations can't be beat.

TIPSTER
Never give just one business card to someone—give him three, at the very least.

Grapevines are for gossip, too

I found my audio-cassette producer in a clubhouse. Okay, I'll admit it, I *was* eavesdropping on his conversation. I heard him talking about himself, so I interrupted and introduced my ideas. Like I said earlier, talk to everyone about your product or service and always be on the prowl for new outlets.

As long as you're on the telephone

Whether you're closing a sale or on a call going nowhere, always ask for a referral, or another contact.

☎ "This may not be a fit here, but you probably know . . . ."

☎ "You know a lot of people in the business. They'd probably want to know about this new technology, too. Anyone come to mind that I could call on?"

☎ "I'm talking to Sports Catalog on the third floor. They're under pressure to meet deadlines, too. Anyone else in the building come to mind?"

☎ "This promotion we're talking about. The banking community is signing up all over town. Anyone come to mind that you think would be interested?"

☎ "We also have a program that works well for young children. The money is set aside for their college funds. Anyone you can think of that should know about it?"

☎ "I understand that you know people in the association. They'll probably want an invitation, too. Any suggestions?"

☎ "Does each division have its own sales department? . . . Do they operate independently of each other? . . . Do you ever talk to one another? . . . Where do you suggest I start?"

☎ "These new programs for small business owners. Any one from the Chamber of Commerce come to mind? . . . We'll need to act quickly. The company will waive the one-time, set-up fee only through the end of the month while we kick off this promotion."

Prospecting is really pretty simple and it can be great fun. People don't work in vacuums, and will often pass along a referral. Whenever I get a new name, I phone right away and use that mutual acquaintance to "warm-up" the cold call . . . "Hi there, so-and-so gave me your name to-day . . . ."

Name, rank, and file'em

Now that you've got your prospects—individuals, small business, big business, whatever the story—draw another dart board so you can rank them. For example, what I often do is have the center of the circle be the person I call when I am ready to close, and each successive circle represents 30 days out, 60 days out, 6 months out.

One more thing. About those seemingly "dead" prospects—keep them somewhere on your list, and stay in touch. They may wake up. Once I nearly gave up on a company, until I heard management had changed hands. To make a long story short, I was able to slip my ideas into the pages of the new owner's business plan.

The wrap-up

Open your mind and your eyes. Get creative when looking for new prospects now that you know what they look like. Hone your networking skills. You're looking for the path of least resistance here. You aren't looking to make this hard on yourself.

Remember, existing customers are prime prospects. Never lose sight of them. It's often easier to collect new business from old customers, than to gather loyal business from strangers. Set daily goals and prospect like mad until you build a list that has no end.

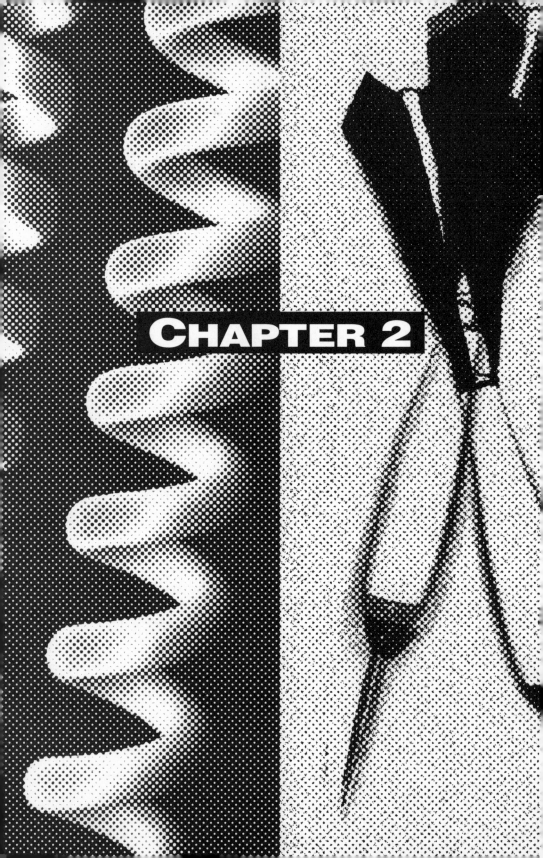

CHAPTER 2

2
What's your story?

Hung up on the wrong line

I received a call from the local cable company last week. The woman sounded professional, and friendly, but she was obviously reading from a script. For more than two minutes she "enlightened" me. Pay $3.95 per month and I can watch the Disney Channel. If I agree today, I get free installation. Twice she said, "Give us a chance."

Now, keep in mind, this cable company has the advantage of name recognition and they are virtually the only game in town. They have a qualified lead list and detailed information about each prospect. This should be a easy sale. But the story was all wrong.

The story that would have sold me was: Disney Channel is now entertaining adults, too. In this cold-caller's place, I would have said, "Hello. This is Joan Guiducci from the Cable Company. I'm calling about a new program that you may want to take advantage of and it costs just

Telephone Talk

TIPSTER

Cold calls fail
when they are
not borne of a
well-focused,
interesting, and
relevant story.

pennies a day. Is this a good time to talk for two minutes?"

"You probably know of the Disney Channel. The programming has taken on some new life. When was the last time you watched their programs?"

If there are no children in the house, I'd point to the changes in programming for older viewers by mentioning a few upcoming shows. You might question further, "Do you have children visiting the house? . . . How often? . . . When they get restless, you can switch on the Disney Channel." The point is, anyone who now subscribes to Disney Channel will be entertained. Disney is affordable and is no longer just for kids.

Sometimes you can abandon your script and just talk to people like they are, well, human beings. Improvise.

Think before you leap

So today, you're promoting a grand new product. This one has legs and is going somewhere fast. You can't wait to begin the flurry of outgoing telephone calls. But hold on. Cold calls only fail because they are not borne of a well-focused, interesting, and relevant story.

Picture a puppy excited about life. She hasn't developed control yet over her paws; the furry feet don't work right, they're cumbersome. The puppy sprawls over the place. Just as clumsy, you hang up from cold calls with a deflated ego and say to yourself, "Well that was lousy. Maybe this isn't the best idea since microwaved bacon." As with most things we do in life, it's important to periodically review our performance. Cold calling is no exception.

When I notice I'm making too many calls with too few results, I stop and sprinkle some introspection into my day. I ask myself questions. Am I calling the right person? Am I asking the right questions? What are they telling me? What am I telling them? I realize I need new words to sell the same old product. So I wipe the slate clean, and reacquaint myself with my product or service and my prospect's profile. Critical to our success as telephone prospectors is understanding our wares and their value, intimately.

Your story behind the story

If you're standing in front of the drawing board, and don't know where to put the first line, consider the way an investigative reporter constructs a front-page story. You'll need a focused idea, the headline, your lead sentence, a picture, and supporting details. Let's work on the idea and the headline.

First, the idea. I would suggest developing a profile that presents your best, and not-so-best sides. Why not sketch a questionnaire for yourself? Brainstorm on a sheet of paper, or into a tape recorder. And pour out whatever comes to mind concerning your product or service.

So back to basics we go. "Who am I? What is my product? What is my expertise? How is my company outstanding? Why should anyone spend money or chant their credit card number for this? Why am I spending time on this phone call? Why should my prospect talk to me? What need does he have that I can fill?" Later, when you're on the phone you'll want to explain, "This is who I am, and this is who I think you are." Spend quality time on these questions and then move on.

Legwork is crucial to building the story. I read trade journals, related newspaper articles, everything I can find that relates or even seems to relate to what I'm selling. I also talk to plenty of people—friend and foe—about the product or service. I make a point to interact with people in my industry. I attend conferences and seminars. This way, I am not just another salesperson, I become a consultant, an expert in the field.

Conversely, research your prospects in the same way. Call for annual reports and brochures. Every bit of background information you have makes your job easier once you're on the telephone.

So read about the product or service, keep your ears open to industry news, trends, and patterns. Pick up key phrases and integrate this new vocabulary into your conversations. Chapter four elaborates on this technique.

I fully believe that knowing your product and company makes up for any self-perceived lack of "telephone talk" talent. Believe me, prospects will listen to what you have to say. These days, people want real and useful information. And that, you've got.

TIPSTER

Knowing your product makes up for any self-perceived lack of "telephone talk" talent.

Search for your *aha!*

It's human nature to sometimes sabotage our strengths and focus on our weaknesses. To get past this paralyzing effect, I like to poke fun at my "inadequacies," reducing them to the ridiculous. I squint at my product and look at it cross-eyed. Well, not literally. The point is to get new perspective. Occasionally, I'll be part of a brilliant conversation, usually when I'm challenged to think about something in a new way. This conversational brilliance can become part of your cold-calling repertoire if you allow that shift of perspective to occur.

Downfalls will metamorphose into windfalls. For example, perhaps you view being a small company in a large industry as a major drawback. Change your mind and decide that "big" can be a liability and "small" is efficient and personable. When you tell your story, your headline will read, "Our prices are fair—we have less overhead than the large companies and you'll get a better value because we work quickly and efficiently, without the bureaucracy." This is a claim, your *aha!*, your headline.

You see, there is something special and unique about your service. When you find it you'll know it. I call it an *aha!* Find it and you pinpoint your place in the world.

A mile in the competition's sneakers

About that niche you're carving. Who shares it with you? Who is the competition? How do they stand out? What are your business parameters, theirs? It's okay to carve a narrow, deep niche—you'll fill it well.

Try listing your accomplishments. How do you set the industry standards? Where has your product been successful and why? How do you overshadow the "other guy"? Are you reviving forgotten courtesies—like door-to-door milk delivery? Do your stores play piano music on every floor?

If you are too humble to answer your own questions, call your loyal customers. They'll tell you why they buy from you.

TIPSTER

It's important to periodically review your performance. So do it.

So what?

But even when you know your product or service intimately, even when you've found your *aha!*, just mentioning facts and features in your cold calling means little until you translate them into living examples. I suggest drawing a mental picture for your prospect to see. Customers don't want to know the virtues of the materials used to make dentures, they want to know they can enjoy eating corn on the cob again.

To determine what benefits to play up, look for the applied value of each feature of your product or service. How will it enhance the personal life or workday of your prospect? What element in that day does it improve? Is your technology better, stronger, faster, safer, or more affordable? How does it affect the prospect's working conditions or life-style?

By listing these elements, you'll begin to build a repertoire of key phrases, points you'll make, questions you'll ask. (I know someone who likes to post cue cards on her computer or bulletin board by the phone.) Try to determine what your customer values, and remember it!

Think about the following ideas—perhaps you can apply them to your situation.

• If you are on the leading edge of technology, perhaps you are passing on savings to the customer.

• You offer a wide selection, something affordable for everyone. People love choice.

• You've serviced the area for 10 years; you are reliable and care about the community.

• Your product can help the prospect get back on schedule and stay within the budget.

• Your computer program makes someone's job more exciting and easier.

Open your mind and view your service as a product

What if you're marketing a service? Treat it like a product. In reviewing the following scenarios, visualize how you can translate your service into product-like features and benefits for prospects.

• What does an event planner actually sell? She sells intangibles like her "connections" and her expertise. But what she really does, is lift the bur-

TIPSTER

If you are too humble to answer your own questions, call your loyal customers. They'll tell you why they buy from you.

den of planning the office Christmas party from a company's secretary who can now spend time attending to company business. And yes, the planner's connections provide the company with the best package for its money. But the most important benefit the event planner provides is that all the company employees have to do is show up. After the party is over, what's left is a memory—a priceless one.

• The carpet cleaning you provide renews the fresh look in someone's home. Carpets stay cleaner, longer.

• A manicurist improves a client's image.

• A diet program sells improved self-esteem. It sells image—its clients look and feel better.

• By offering a similar service for less money, your prospect can spend the money saved on lunch for himself and a friend.

Some words to get you started

Here is the result of my brainstorm of words that I use to get my story started:

specialize, expertise, well-known, personable, caring, successful, accomplished, connections, loyal, niche, creative, unique, leading-edge, special, best, innovative, recent, new, proven, latest, industry-standard, trend, breakthrough, enhance, superior, satisfaction, reliable, streamlined, effective, efficient, accurate, selection, choice, flexible, control, opportunity, stronger, productive, improve, replace, growth, powerful, better, easy, effortless, faster, speed, quickly, increase, growing, more, less, fewer, eliminate, reduce, equal, savings, results, affordable, fair, reasonable, value, total quality, and on, and on.

After you've said "hello"

You've targeted your prospect, and you've constructed a well-rounded story for yourself. But you still face dialing the phone—cold. Your prospect will be interrupted, and you've got to warm him up within the first 7 to 10 seconds.

Here's a technique that always works for me. I use a couple of sentences that help me ease both parties into conversation. I call these phrases "warm-ups." Your warm-up is a move toward common ground. It's a common denominator you and your prospect share, and it's not necessarily product related. It's stretching your hamstring muscles before the sprint.

A warm-up may involve:
- your accomplishments.
- public opinion.
- a third-party opinion.
- a newspaper article.
- a common denominator.
- growing or fading trends.
- a simple observation or knowledge you have.
- follow up on a direct mailer, or on a convention.
- product claim.

TIPSTER
Your warm-up is a reach for familiar ground. It's stretching your hamstring muscles before the sprint.

You gather warm-ups as you prospect from referrals, or from building your contact list. Here are some ideas based on the above list to get you started after you say hello and introduce yourself.

- Mention your accomplishments (now is not the time to be shy).
    ☎ **"We're one of the best in the area at . . . ."**
    ☎ **"You may know us from the work we did for . . . ."**
    ☎ **"If you know . . . then you probably know of our work."**
    ☎ **"We received an award for our work with . . . ."**

- Announce special ratings by neutral third parties.
    ☎ **"The Chamber of Commerce published a survey placing us as one of the top five companies in town for customer satisfaction."**

- Connect with follow-ups.
    ☎ **"We spoke at the dental trade show about writing your newsletter. This type of quarterly contact shows your patients you care, keeps them informed on the latest in cosmetic**

TIPSTER
Tap into
yourself and find
out what you
can offer people.

dentistry, and keeps your patient base healthy."

☎ "I mailed the information you requested. Have you taken time to review the benefits? . . . I'd like to point out a couple of issues."

☎ "There was so much excitement at the seminar, I'd like to speak to you now, while it's quiet."

• Mention media coverage.

☎ "I'm sure you read about us in the *Rochester Daily* business section."

• Recall headlines.

☎ "You may have seen the recent news in the press about carpal tunnel syndrome. Doctors say everyone typing for more than 4 hours daily is affected. We've developed a product to reduce the pain for your employees and save you money on worker's compensation."

• Offer diverse selection.

☎ "We understand these volatile economic times, but people love to feel healthy. That's why we offer fitness club memberships to fit every budget—from $200 to $2,000."

• Find a common denominator.

☎ "We live in the same neighborhood."

☎ "We know the same people."

☎ "We belong to the same club."

☎ "I'm calling about an innovative program we've designed for small business owners like you. Our clients are telling us how much time they're saving."

• Extol the virtues of your business or who you are.

☎ "We're big on quality, reasonable on cost."

☎ "Sure, we're small, but we maintain loyal customers

because we work hard to take care of them. Let us take care of you too."

☎ "Since we don't know each other, I'd like to tell you about myself and the kind of work I do."

☎ "I specialize in providing catering services for small business owners . . . I have spent the last 5 years working with . . . ."

☎ "I'm good at developing other people's ideas into a tangible product."

- State what prompted you to call.

    ☎ "I've been watching your company grow for the last few years. My background may be of some interest to you."

    ☎ "I was driving through the neighborhood yesterday and noticed your house. The landscaping really stands out."

- Use a personal touch. Mention what you know about the person or company you're calling.

    ☎ "I understand your son is going to college this fall. You may want to know about the recent increase of interested buyers in your neighborhood."

    ☎ "I noticed the article about your company in yesterday's *Journal*. It occurred to me that you may be interested in our services."

- Inform your prospect about herself, if you have the research.

    ☎ "I understand you are self-employed, and you make plenty of in-state phone calls in the normal working day . You qualify for a plan allowing for 3 hours of free long distance every month."

    ☎ "I've studied your account and have some ideas that can save you money."

☎ "I understand you work on a computer for at least 6 hours every day. The glare can be damaging your eyesight. Have you considered using a nonglare screen to reduce possible eyesight injury?"

☎ "We've conducted a market analysis of houses in your neighborhood. You may be amazed by the results. I'm able to get you a complimentary copy of the study. When was the last time you spoke to someone about the market value of your home?"

- Mention how you got the prospect's name.

    ☎ "Bob Summers and I are talking about a new program. He thinks you may be interested as well."

    ☎ "You may know of us through our association with Midwest Bank."

- Say something to close the gap in that first 7 seconds.

    ☎ "I didn't want to overlook anyone."

    ☎ "I think you'll be interested in knowing about this."

    ☎ "I wanted personally to talk to you."

    ☎ "A neighbor is getting great results. It occurred to me that you'd want to be involved in this."

The wrap-up

I suggest spending time with cold callers who interrupt your day. What do these people say? And how do you react? Naturally, if a call doesn't relate to you, you won't be interested. Put yourself on the receiving end. Just as you now study junk mail, listen to cold callers and learn what to do and what not to do.

Continue honing your story and collecting warm-ups. Life is fluid and you must act accordingly. So be flexible. Knowing your position, you'll respond to the obvious and learn from the unexpected, for the next time around.

All of this planning for a few minutes of phone talk? Yes. Planning puts substance into every number you dial. Carefully chosen words, used in the right order, bring results.

CHAPTER 3

3
Blueprint for a successful cold call

Plan your work and work your plan

By now, you're quick-witted about the product or service and ready to tell your prospect just enough to nudge him to the next stage. But amid your enthusiasm for selling your product, have you been pouring on the gravy before serving the meat and potatoes? Perhaps you muddle through somehow, making your prospect feel uncomfortable and irritated. And if you've ended up grasping for words, you may also have ended up suggesting your product isn't very good. A contemplated strategy is critical to getting the most from your phone call. Give your prospect a plate first, then move from point A to B to C, serving logically.

Like a memorable meal, a successful cold call has a beginning, middle and end.

Before the beginning

My sixth grade teacher suggested my essays be as long as a piece of string. A piece of string is cut just long or short enough to do the job. Thus, the length of your cold call should be as long as it takes to tell the story; as long as a piece of string.

How many minutes you spend on each cold call is in part determined by your objective, which you must define before beginning the call. Are you setting an appointment, taking sales orders, gathering facts, conducting an interview or survey, sending literature for follow up, registering someone for a seminar, or determining a prospect's budget for a project? Naturally, each task requires its own timetable.

So your objective outlines the shape of your script. Map your questions so that the conversation closes where you want it to. Through your questions and answers, you'll be on the alert for signs of resistance or commitment. Depending on the circumstances, avoid telling too much on the first call. Accomplish your objective, and then hang up. Create some intrigue. Leave your prospect excited about the meeting, information, or whatever.

Can't say it

If you're unable to pronounce a prospect's name, don't fake it. Many people resent their names mutilated. Just say "Hello, I'm calling for Joan . . . it looks like I'm going to have a hard time with this last name, can you help me out?" This approach reveals your human side.

Or if you're introducing a new technology, say, "I can barely pronounce this one, do you have a pencil, you should write this down." This technique encourages your contact to be actively involved in the call.

Telephone Talk

And get to the point

Be personable, but not personal. Save the dawdling chatter filled with "how are you" for your sister. Prospects aren't about to reveal their true physical or emotional status. Would you really want them to? But when your dialogue is engaging, you give each contact a cue to communicate.

By practicing sincerity, you'll create interest for keeping in touch.

However, you may be personal with referrals from friends, because you'll call on that inherent, personal flavor. And later on as you come to know your prospects, and they become tried and true clients, by all means, get a little more personal with people. That's okay.

This is who I am, this is who I think you are

So now you've dialed the number and reached your contact. Slowly introduce yourself (don't rush your name). Say who your are, and where you are from. If I am calling from out of town, or long distance, I say so. You'll notice this technique creates a sense of urgency.

To avoid wasting time talking to the wrong person, I always remember to confirm the contact's responsibilities. You should, too.

TIPSTER

Your cold call should be as long as a piece of string—long enough to do the job.

☎ **"I understand that you're involved in managing the administrative side of the business. Is that correct?"**

☎ **"I understand you're in the accounting department. Perhaps you can help me. Who makes the decision for purchasing software?"**

Create intrigue with warm-ups

The time you have to grab your prospects attention is narrow—7 to 10 seconds. A good way to invite someone to hang up on you, or cut you off, is by immediately segueing into a monologue or reading directly from a script. For now, concentrate on bringing your contact into the conversation. I suggest warming up the conversation with a sentence or two.

☎ **"I understand that . . . ."**

☎ **"I phoned you especially to talk about . . . ."**

☎ **"I've heard your name mentioned a few times today."**

☎ **"You may know us from the district. We've been in the Haverfeld building for over 10 years now. It's been a long time since we talked to you. A lot has happened in the last few years that you may want to know about."**

☎ "We've taken a unique approach to home alarm systems. Others in your neighborhood are installing now, and saving money while they build their homes."

☎ "John Yee suggested that I speak to you, so I called right away because I didn't want to overlook anyone."

When you refer to a third party's opinion or results, you'll be more credible.

Can we talk now?

Believe me, you're going to encounter people who are a little bit rough around the edges. A red flag goes up as soon as you hear their voices. My suggestion for working effectively with such people is to be polite and firm. Be sensitive that this person may be working under a deadline, may have received some bad news, had too many cold calls, whatever. You might come out and say, "This doesn't sound like a good time for you." Attempting to be aware of a prospect's situation will soften the grumble. Often you can actually hear your prospect sigh, when he says, "It really isn't a good time. What is this all about?"

You might say, "It's best we talk when you have more time. I have an idea you might want to know about. I didn't want to overlook anyone. How does your schedule look for this afternoon?" You can usually find out when your prospect will have an extra 5 or 10 minutes. You really want his full attention. Set a time to call back.

"Sounds like you've got a few distractions now, perhaps I'll call back this afternoon. Is three o'clock all right with you?"

And then return the call when you said you would. Red-flag cases aside, most people are available to hear your story. So your warm-up must be provocative. Why? Because afterwards, when you ask, "Is this a good time to talk?" your prospect will be interested enough to savor a few moments with a new idea. Otherwise, this question provides a comfortable way out for your prospects.

One way to grab attention is to say, "Is this a good time to talk for just 2 minutes?" Prospects appreciate the limit you've set for telling your story, so they'll usually carve out 120 seconds from their schedule.

Telephone Talk

TIPSTER

The time slot you have to grab your prospect's attention is narrow—7 to 10 seconds.

Make sure you tell your story in 2 minutes. Keep your promise. Let your prospect spill into overtime.

Don't begin in the middle

Of course, you'll want to tell your prospects what you do best, but not all at once. Have you ever found yourself asking for the order before you've proven your case? Of course, and how often did you get it?

Let's go back. Remember when you were honing your story, and targeting prospects, you painted big-picture ideas and then funneled down to the details? I would take the same approach during the cold call. After introducing myself, warming up the conversation, and asking for a few moments of telephone time, I make my claim. I paint that big-picture concept.

In other words, start with the broad description (usually two or three sentences) of your product or service, emphasizing the value of each feature. Then ask a question to determine level of interest and need. Try tailoring your claim to the concerns of each individual, and slant your language toward each person, too.

TIPSTER
Be personable,
but not
personal.

☎ "I understand you're involved in manufacturing. We have a productivity tool that can shorten production time and testing by at least 60 percent. When do you transfer processing?"

☎ "This is Mary Lou Abbott of ABC Company in San Francisco. I understand that you manage the shipping department. We've developed the latest technology for firms in your field. You may be spending a lot of dollars unnecessarily. We can help you save money. How are you tracking your orders?"

☎ "I understand you order your company's office supplies. The International Association of Stamp Collectors has endorsed our 12-color fax machines because they solve the problem of transmitting subtle colors and designs. We believe we can show you similar results. What are you using now?"

When stating your claim, understate rather than overstate.

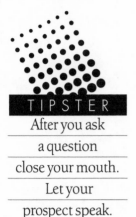

TIPSTER
After you ask
a question
close your mouth.
Let your
prospect speak.

Overstatement may be viewed as a sales ploy. The sincere approach will transform qualified prospects into buyers.

More warm-ups and claims

☎ "I'm calling about the health of you and your patients. What do you do with your dental instruments after they have been used? . . . We're introducing a sterilization process for instruments we think you should know about it. So we're offering a free seminar to doctors in your building. How does your schedule look on . . . ?"

☎ "We have a special promotion through the end of this month. Big savings for you. We're getting a strong response from other hospitals in the area. I thought you would want to know about our program."

• Suppose you've received a request for more information based on an advertisement you ran in a magazine. You might follow up with:

☎ "I understand that you saw our ad in the *City Journal*. I've been talking to a lot of people about it for the last week. What's your interest in . . . ?"

• Or suppose you were canvassing door to door last week:

☎ "I stopped by your office the other day. You were in a meeting. I left some information. Have you had time to read it? . . . I'd like to point out a couple of items you might be interested in."

• Say you've had great success in a market:

☎ "We have a program that's being warmly received in the legal community. We've signed up several law firms in your part of town. I didn't want to overlook anyone."

- Or you've read about your prospect in the local paper:

  ☎ **"I noticed the article about your company in yesterday's paper. It occurred to me that you might be interested in our services."**

- Suppose you gathered names from an open house:

  ☎ **"We closed the sale on a house right down the block from you. They're quite pleased with the offer. We still have a list of buyers interested in owning homes in your neighborhood. I think we should talk . . ."**

- If you've just opened your business, you might say:

  ☎ **"We just opened our doors last week at Fifth Avenue and Main Street. I called to tell you about our plans to support the neighborhood. I'd like to give you a personal tour. How does your schedule look on Friday?"**

- Introduce yourself with a direct-mail campaign and then follow up with a telephone call.

  ☎ **"I'm calling about a letter we sent you last week about our program. Has it come across your desk yet? . . . I'd like to point out a couple of items."**

Questions, questions

Asking questions makes you seem professional, and of course, you are a professional. Your cold call is the time to engage in conversation, and hopefully, it kicks off a new business relationship. But ask just enough to accomplish your objective. During the call, you are controlling what your prospect thinks and talks about.

First, you want to open the dialogue. Yes or no questions can be limiting. Ask a relevant question, one that will push the conversation further. You are beginning the process of finding "need"; so go ahead, probe and qualify this prospect.

TIPSTER

Be sensitive
when greeting
a grumpy prospect.
She may be
working under a
deadline, too.

Telephone
Talk

For example, if you are selling check-writing software, you might ask, "How many checks do you write in a month?" If the answer is "three," this prospect doesn't need what you're selling. In this case, next I'd ask, "Do you expect that to change?" I'd note the response and follow up in 3 or 4 months.

Your second line of questioning lets you make points about your product or service, and allows the prospect an opportunity to voice an opinion. Say a prospect tells you he processes two hundred checks per month. You ask, "How much time does that take? . . . Well, let me tell you about what we can do for you."

The further you question, the more opportunity you have to fill in details. Remember the funnel metaphor. First you present big-picture concepts and then add the particulars. At this point in the dialogue, you're ready to particularize. I suggest asking open-ended and positive questions to continue productive dialogue. Your word choice is also very important. Consider the different answers to these two questions. How is the decision made? Who signs the contract? The first will open dialogue. The second will bring the specific answer you need.

Build a list for yourself, and place it by the telephone. Here are some ideas.

☎ "Tell me about . . ."

☎ "Did you read . . . ?"

☎ "What is your opinion?"

☎ "What are your thoughts?"

☎ "How many . . . ?"

☎ "When is the last time you spoke to someone about . . ?"

☎ "What are your plans . . . ?"

☎ "What are you doing about . . . ?"

☎ "How have you approached the problem of . . . ?"

☎ "Have there ever been discussions about . . . ?"

☎ "Have you ever heard of . . . ? Basically, it's used for . . . ."

☎ "How would you describe the way you're doing . . . ?"

☎ "Have you considered . . . ?"

☎ "Does your staff ever ask about . . . ?"

☎ "Have you given any thought to . . . ?"

☎ "When do you think this will change?"

☎ "How much have you budgeted for this? . . . Are those funds available now?"

☎ "What cost would you be comfortable with?"

☎ "When do you expect to add this to your budget?"

☎ "Do you feel comfortable with . . . ?"

Sometimes you just have to go ahead and ask a hard question. The two most challenging queries to pose are:

☎ "Do you have the money in your budget?"

☎ "Are you interested in this?"

Now. Listen up. When you ask a question, don't answer for the prospect. Stay quiet and give her time to think and respond. I know it's hard to reign in your enthusiasm, but let the prospect speak and finish her point.

One more thing (I call it active listening). Have you ever felt as if someone dropped the phone and walked away while you were talking? If you have, then you realize you must let people know you are there listening. Provide subtle encouragement like "Oh, I've heard that," "Yes, I agree," "Uh huh, I follow," "That's interesting."

These little phrases elicit more "telephone talk," which is what you want (or you wouldn't have bought this book). You'll be surprised how easily the conversation flows and how much information you gather using this approach.

I'm not interested. Am I?

Prospects are too valuable. They cost too much time and money to find and cultivate for you to fail because you didn't plan a tight presentation, to flinch upon hearing the slightest mention of "no." You have to learn to reframe the definition of "objection equals rejection."

First, find out if it is indeed an objection. Restate what was said to you, and rephrase the question.

"Let me see if I understand you correctly. Are you saying . . . ?"

And if it's valid, view this resistance as a sign of interest, a call for more information. Do yourself and your business a favor. Turn your weaknesses into strengths. If you don't believe me, just decide that for 1 day of telephone prospecting, when you hear an objection, you'll offer more details.

"I understand your point of view. Let me tell you about some changes that are happening. Someone in your building had the same concern until . . . ."

Resistance comes in all shapes. Make a list of objections you've heard or expect to hear from prospects, such as:

"I don't do business with people I don't know."

"I'm not interested."

"I can't afford that."

"We don't need that."

Do this and you'll be ready with a list of answers.

☎ **"I may be young and new to the area, but I assure you I have fresh ideas, a different perspective than people of a different generation."**

☎ **"I'm schooled in the latest technology, where others may be using outdated, old-fashioned methods to achieve similar results. I can save you money."**

☎ **"I may be smaller than big business, but I am less expensive, don't carry much overhead, and can give you the personal attention you deserve."**

• Suppose you're a veteran, with many successful years in your industry; you might respond to the objection with:

☎ **"We've made some changes in our service. We've added the latest technology. And we're able to pass the savings on to you. You'll be pleased with the results you'll get."**

No means maybe, sometimes

Many prospects say "no" to a question they thought they heard. Just as you reframe objections, rephrase your questions.

If you're engaged in a telephone call that is not going anywhere,

TIPSTER

An objection is not a rejection. It's a call for more information.

it's not necessarily a fault of your approach. Anything is possible. Perhaps your prospect's wife sells a competitive product. At any rate, you don't want to beat a dead cow. Perhaps this person really doesn't need your service. You'll recognize this and ask for a referral before you move forward. For example, a telephone prospector calling for an insurance company, may gather information and then say, "Sounds like you're well covered, is there anyone you know who might need . . . ?"

But also keep in touch with "dead" prospects. Don't be intrusive, but check in occasionally. Sometimes when you call people over 3 or 4 months they begin to feel a need for your product or service.

Avoid the know-it-all syndrome

Pretending you know something, when you don't, just won't work in cold calling. Don't be afraid to say, "I don't know. But I'll find out and get back to you."

I relish the times when a prospect asks a question. I remember a friend of mine who changed careers, moving from retail clothing into high-tech electronic sales. She played the role of front person for products she didn't totally understand. She placed cold calls to senior managers, presented big-picture ideas, and put prospects through a rigorous qualifying process. When the "techies" returned her calls, she'd shift gears. No way could she address these complicated matters. But her inadequacies worked in her favor. If a prospect expressed serious interest in what she was selling, she knew. It was time to pass the ball to someone else. Her approach went like this:

"That's a good question. I've made a note to get an answer for you. It also occurs to me that we have something you'd like to know a lot more about. I'd like you to talk with Suzanne Ishimaru; she's our specialist. Let's set aside some time for all of us to meet in person. I'll put some information into the mail for you to review before the meeting."

At times—when you don't want your prospect to know everything you know—it's okay to be vague about some details. Sometimes

Telephone Talk

TIPSTER
Be sure to
stay in touch
with your
prospects.

you don't want to answer all the questions. Hold on to ways to stay in touch.

Hang up and regroup

In the coming chapters I'll encourage you to maintain a fresh appeal, to treat each cold call as if it were the first one of the day. Do this and your quiet confidence will show through in your voice. But there will be times when you hear your voice wavering or feel your energy evaporating. At these times, set aside your prospect list until your spirits lift again. It's okay to get tired. Acknowledge that it's part of the business and allow yourself to regroup. Do something else or call someone familiar. I'll often call an associate or client to bask in the security of a familiar business relationship.

Dead air closing in

Ever feel the conversation dulling, losing its edge? Your prospect sighs, and then you squirm through extended silence. You know the interaction is breaking down, and that's a major clue to pull the conversation together and close the call. This is not to say that you wait for the dead air to close in. Instinct will tell you when it's closing time. Remember the piece of string.

☎ "I think we have a fit here, we should talk more. How does your schedule look on . . ."

☎ "I'd like to fax you some information we can talk about . . . It's only two pages, but full of valuable ideas and options for you. Let's set a telephone date for 2 P.M on Thursday."

☎ "I'll be in your neighborhood next Wednesday. I'm sure I can show you a way to cut back significantly on your expenses. How does your schedule look?"

☎ "I don't think this is right for you at the moment. When do you see your situation changing?"

☎ "I think I may have something for you, but I need to do some research. I'll be back in touch next Wednesday with that information. How does your calendar look?"

☎ "I'll put our catalogue in the mail. May I check with you from time to time."

☎ "I'll pencil you in on the seminar schedule and get that fax to you now. Tomorrow I'll call to confirm and to sign up anyone else who might be interested."

☎ "So, I'll see you Saturday at 10 A.M. And you have my number in case something comes up in the meantime."

Both of you agree on a plan of action. You may be setting an appointment, signing someone up for a seminar, or sending literature and following up next week. Use fax machines when possible. The fax suggests urgency and importance. Be sure to confirm the next step, summarize the phone call, and thank the contact for her time.

And furthermore

Remember, you're in control of when you call, of the points you make, of what you ask, of the pace you take, and of how you close. Avoid reading from a script or talking too much. If you're speaking, you're not learning.

Concentrate on being clear. Clarity is the key to success. Move from big to little. You'll have plenty of time for the particulars. Think of your cold call as an inverted pyramid.

And as I've mentioned before, preparation will compensate for your self-perceived "lack of telephone talk." You'll know you can respond to questions and objections, and you will.

TIPSTER

Put aside
your prospect list
until your
spirits lift.

The wrap-up

Before you dial the telephone number:
- target your prospects.
- hone your story.
- separate ideas into the big-picture and the details.
- determine your outcome, keep in mind your objectives. Are you on a fact-finding mission, taking orders, setting appointments, conducting an interview, or sending out literature for follow-up?
- review your notes and plan your conversation. And keep documents at hand.
- summarize your questions and comments and keep them in front of you.

During the call:
- introduce yourself: this is who I am, this is who I think you are.
- warm up the conversation, pique curiosity and create goodwill.
- ask if this is a good time to talk; if not, set a time to call back.
- state your claim, slanting benefits toward each contact's concerns.
- ask open-ended questions and continue productive conversation.
- overcome objections by understanding the resistance and then stress benefits over features.
- attain your objective and begin the wrap-up, which should confirm your plan of action.
- ask for referrals or more contacts before you hang up.
- know when to close, and do it quickly after expressing thanks.

After the call:
- follow through on your plan of action.
- keep accurate notes.
- review your performance.

P.S. After you've reached your daily goal, say to yourself, "I'll make just one more call." You'll be amazed at how relaxed you'll be and how good you'll feel for stretching your limits.

CHAPTER 4

4

Who's the boss?

No such thing as a one-man band

Even if you land a meeting with the President of the United States (an ultimate decision maker), he still must consult his advisers, or his wife, before giving the final buy signal.

Protect yourself and don't be the salesperson who only meets the manager to sell the concept and sign on the dotted line. If you rely on one person's opinion, you leave yourself wide open for trouble.

Suppose you sold a computer system to a company without talking to end-users. Those employees may sabotage the system after installation. And that reflects on the sales person. While some people don't have the authority to say yes, they can say no to a corporate decision. I have learned this lesson at some expense. Talk to all the people who will be involved in using your product or service.

What do you do for a living?

Makes me chuckle when I think of it now, but a while ago, when I was selling software by telephone, my mistake wasn't so funny.

The bosses handed all the cold and lukewarm accounts to me. I was to take a deep breath and sell, sell, sell. I was instructed to "get a copy of the software into the system manager's office."

Within two weeks, dozens of system managers across the country were mailed a sample product. Disaster ensued.

In nearly every case, the system manager's job description was not quite what I had in mind. He or she was the custodian of the computer system, and not the decision maker. I had been dealing with people too low on the totem pole. And to tell you the truth, I think I knew it all along. For some reason, I ignored that voice tugging inside me. To be frank, my mistake was failing to ask two critical questions: "How do you fit in at the company? Who else is involved in these decisions?"

I lost precious time catching up with all my test sites and as a result the mistake cost me thousands of dollars in sales. Again, the moral of the foible—talk to everyone involved in the decision. And always ask a contact just how he or she fits into the organization.

Reinventing the wheel

Picture a bicycle wheel. The center represents the ultimate decision maker. Each spoke is a person who will somehow influence the decision to buy or not to buy, and each will give a green or red light for the purchase. In most sales, you'll find more than one person affects the outcome. I call this the "buying group." The more complex the sale, the more "spokes" I speak with.

Make it your goal to personally speak with each "spoke" about issues important to his or her position. You may even draw a diagram labeling managers, financial people, legal advisers, end-users and computer experts, and so on. If it's a product for the home, you might list family members, friends, and neighbors.

The simple—but not so easy—sale

Let's open the window on a young couple buying their dream home. Both husband and wife must see the view, the hardwood floors, the French doors. To make the sale, you must aim to collect agreement from each—individually, and then together. You'll tune in to the concerns of each person.

This wife needs a room to run her party-planning business, and the husband insists on having a large, modern kitchen. And don't forget their five-year-old daughter.

You make one of probably dozens of calls and say to the wife, "I found a house with a room that's perfect for your office—airy and spacious, with plenty of sunshine. By the way, tell Mr. Parker about the kitchen. It's got yards of Corian countertops. I think you'll both be pleased with the financing the owners have agreed to. Oh, and tell Maggie there's a sandbox and a swing set in the back yard."

You've tried to address everyone's concern in a personable way. Hopefully, you've encouraged dialogue among the decision makers, and soothed them with picturesque ideas.

Corporate decisions, complex sales

Consider the many spokes in a company: CEO, managers, accountants, stockholders, end-users, technical specialists, personnel, secretaries. I've also discovered that the more people I speak to within an organization, the more successful I am at getting the business, or closing the deal.

Here's some advice. Think of yourself as a project manager. The sale is not a linear process. One thing doesn't necessarily follow the other. Consider lead times. Get the gears meshed and soon you become part of the organization. Not one person in the company is going to carry your idea. You'll be in all departments, walking your talk.

I once promoted a hardware and software product, claiming it

TIPSTER

Tailor your claims to the concern of each individual.

improved customer service. The technology was sophisticated. It compiled trends, produced reports, and rapidly retrieved information.

Not knowing exactly where to begin, I called customer service and introduced myself and the product to the manager. He was interested, so I set my plan of action and made an appointment with him.

But before I hung up, I said, "I understand that you have a night shift. Does the supervisor report to you? . . . You must work closely together. Should we set a meeting later in the day to include him?"

And if I'd done all my homework, I'd have also asked:

"How would you go about discussing this with your operators? . . . Should one sit in on the meeting?"

"This is a big decision for the company. How is it made? . . . Who are the people involved? . . . How do they fit in to the decision making process?"

"What groups are on the distribution list for reports? . . . Who reads them?"

"What groups would support the equipment purchase?"

"How is the technical review made? . . . Are there specialists involved? . . . What are their needs and expectations?"

More, more, and more contacts

Set to work building a list of people influencing the sale, then address their concerns, clarify their opinions. All the while, dig for new contacts, moving through the company, up and down the ladder and across the board.

☎ "I'm talking to Bert Adams about engineering reports and Cheryl Brigham in finance. Have I overlooked anyone?"

☎ "Do you know of others that I should be talking to? I wouldn't want to overlook anyone."

☎ "It occurred to me that manufacturing should hear about our plan. Where do you suggest I start?"

☎ "I understand Barbara Hunt makes the financial decisions. Whom does she rely on to review programs?"

☎ "I should talk to someone in the purchasing department about how to handle the paperwork. Where do you suggest I start?"

☎ "Who else in the company does he talk to about these matters?"

When you can't reach an important "spoke," speak to her secretary. Tell him about your project.

☎ "I'm having trouble getting through to Mark Wright. He's working on a deadline now. Any suggestion on someone else I could start with?"

☎ "Perhaps you can help me. I've been calling Jane Runak since last week. She must be very busy. We're organizing a presentation. I'm sure she'd like to know about it. Perhaps we can include someone else from the group. What do you suggest I do?"

☎ "I'm calling her about . . . . Is there anyone else you suggest I speak to?"

Make a habit of assuring each contact by saying, "I'll contact these people on my own, so I won't interrupt your busy schedule."

Rollin', rollin', rollin'

Telephone Talk

To keep myself optimistic about a complex sale, and to maintain momentum, I contact people as soon as I get their names. And you should too. And remember to introduce yourself with a warm-up with each department you call.

"I'm talking to Don Ride in customer service about a new program. He told me to call you about . . . "

Next, I might call engineering and say, "I understand you review the monthly report. I'd like to know more about how you implement that information, and what other data your department may be looking for."

Then I inevitably talk to accounts payable:

"We're outlining some savings here. I don't want to overlook any other options we should consider. I understand that you can fill me in on the telephone billing system."

Then systems support:

"It occurred to me that we should talk to you about our plans with customer support. We've got some ideas on the support they need. We'd like to find out more about what you need."

Remember to talk about your product from each "spoke's" point of view.

Court the champions

A champion is an insider who stands to gain something—prestige, recognition, or whatever—from supporting your program and defending your cause. She's someone you encounter who works on your behalf, who supports your product, or your service. Keep her advised of your progress and use her as a reference. Cultivate these kinds of relationships. You can never have too many of them.

☎ "We're making good progress. I'd like to fill you in . . ."

☎ "I am speaking to a woman on the same block. She's interested in our program. She'd like to talk to someone in the neighborhood using the service. Your name came to mind. Would you have time to speak with her?"

☎ "I'm talking to John Lu about our service. He's also a member of the Metro User Group. You've had such great results with us. Increases in productivity and so forth. Is it possible for you to talk to him about . . . ?"

Remember to return the favor, champions need support, too.

☎ "I heard from Jerry Kurt the other day. He has great respect for your opinion. We have a meeting set for next Wednesday. I understand the results you are getting are more than you ever expected. We really appreciate your support."

Ask for assistance in moving through an organization.

☎ "I'm looking for some advice. With all the talk in the papers about the new plant opening in the spring, it occurred to me that . . . . Any ideas on how I might get started?"

Beware of blockers

Sometimes your sales progress skids to a halt. We've all met more blockers than we'd care to. Some are assigned by the company to filter services, the way personnel screens candidates for job openings. Others are self-appointed authorities. Some insist on being your only contact in the company. Sound familiar?

I like to put them at ease, by working with them, if I can. On a job hunt, you've probably tried to slide through a back door to the department with the job opening, and heard, "I'd love to talk to you directly but you have to go through the proper channels."

To this I'd respond, "Maybe you can fill me in on the kind of person you'd like in the group. Personnel is often only interested in credentials. I find there's so much more than that."

In your mind, separate gatekeepers from blockers, although both may say, "We don't want any." Circumvent blockers when you can. And know when to walk away. But be persistent, things will often go your way.

It never hurts to test the waters and say, "I didn't know you made those decisions for the company. How do you fit in? . . . Maybe we should meet." Say this in a light spirit, without arrogance, and you'll probably avoid any bad feelings.

Beware of the man who beats his own drum. He's easy to recognize. "The company always relies on my advice with these issues," he'll say. When I come across a blocker like this, I revel in asking questions he can't answer so he'll connect me with people who can. This reduces the blocker's self-appointed authority.

TIPSTER

The more people you speak to within an organization, the more successful you'll be closing the sale.

In other cases, I take my blocker by the hand and lead him down my path of reason. For example, if I am trying to gather names, my strategy is to ask how decisions are made and about the people who are affected. You want him to give way to a larger circle of players. Here's a series of questions and statements:

☎ **"Do you make these decisions alone ? . . . With whom do you consult?"**

☎ **"Whom do you rely on for advice about . . . ?"**

TIPSTER
Telephone new contacts as soon as you get their names.

☎ "How is . . . planned?"

☎ "How is it approved?"

☎ "What groups are affected by this?"

☎ "Maybe we should discuss this issue with people from that work group. We wouldn't want to overlook anything that might come up later."

☎ "We might gather some good ideas if we invite people from accounting. They are usually quite helpful with their questions and concerns."

☎ "So and so waited until the end before talking to end-users. That was quite a setback. Maybe we should get them involved right away."

Which spoke do I pick?

Corporations can resemble amoebas, amorphous, not clearly structured. So where do you begin? If you're selling supplies, like copier paper or computer disks, talk to the purchasing department.

Selling a service? Contact the department that would most benefit from your work. Human resources contracts with temporary agencies. Property management contracts with architects, janitorial services, and sign painters. Experience and instinct will help you here.

This is the operator

Try the main switchboard even if you've had a sour experience with operators. They really can be helpful. I have a colleague who needed the names of 104 marketing and human resource directors in northern California corporations—not an easy task, he thought. He hired a bright, friendly sounding college freshman to call each company. To his surprise, sometimes the operator offered the name, sometimes the caller was referred to a department. Within three days, the list contained 86 names. In some places, operators will give you the breakdown on who reports to whom.

Treat every gatekeeper with respect. If you call cold and don't identify yourself, you'll encounter a lot of resistance, especially if you immediately ask for information.

Jumping in and saying, "Who's the vice president of engineering?" won't get you results. Try the following:

"Hello, this is Susan Cook from Point Press in Ohio. I'm putting a package in the mail for the director of human resources, could you tell me his name?" If you encounter resistance, be quick on your toes. Say something like, "My boss gave me the name and I've misplaced it. Can you help me out?"

When all you have is a contact's telephone number

Many directories or lists you buy just provide the company name and CEO's number, at most. And many times, you don't need to speak with the man in charge.

There will be times when you don't have a contact name. To find the person with whom you need to speak, decide the information you need to know, and move to the company's department that might answer your questions.

What is your plan of action? Do you want to hang up with a scheduled appointment, or just the manager's name? What system does the company currently use, and how it is working? Is there talk of upgrading the system? Are you going to send literature and agree to talk next week? Be sure to list key phrases, questions to ask, points to make, and what you want to accomplish during the call.

I've found end-users very helpful if you use their jargon. Use their time wisely, get the information you need, and move on. And remember, when you make some cold calls, try viewing them as surveys, or interviews, rather than sales calls. When approached this way, people are naturally more talkative. In this case, dial directly into the department that might use your product, introduce yourself and then probe.

☎ **"We're interested in your reaction to . . . ."**
☎ **"Describe your approach to . . . ."**
☎ **"How are you doing that now?"**
☎ **"Anything you'd like to change?"**
☎ **"Tell me about your current system."**

TIPSTER
Cultivate relationships with champions, you can never have too many.

☎ "Have you considered . . . ?"

☎ "Who would be the best person for me to start talking with? . . . And how does she fit in?"

☎ "Perhaps you can help me locate someone in the department. We have a system that . . . ."

I rarely begin at the top of the ladder. First, I'll gather information from within, so I'm better prepared to make my presentation to the CEO, if need be. I'll often build my case by determining the company's needs from the bottom and mid–levels of the organization.

TIPSTER

Dig for new
contacts. Move
through the
company—up and
down the ladder
and across the
board.

The wrap-up

Always find out who is involved in making the final decisions. Know who signs the contracts. Determine how each "spoke" fits in. Understand the nature of his issues and concerns. Sometimes internal politics can sabotage, halt or hinder the sales process. This is why I suggest talking to a lot of people.

CHAPTER 5

5

Leave a message, but don't hang up

They know who you are

Once I retrieved this call from my message machine: "Hello, this is Sergeant Byrd from the Police Department. Please call me at 585-2222." You can bet I called him immediately. As it turned out, no, I didn't want tickets to the policemen's ball, but his message was highly effective. I quickly returned his call because I recognized the organization and wanted to know what they wanted.

If you're fortunate enough to work for a well-known name like IBM or General Mills, people will probably return your call.

Also, your current clients will usually call you back. And because they know you and your style, you don't necessarily have to leave creative messages.

The way to recognize and develop message skills, is to start listening to messages left for you by people you don't know. Think about

TIPSTER

Start listening
to messages left
by people you
don't know.

your own priorities. You probably return calls to the cable company, the bank, the phone company. Which cold calls do you return? Which messages do you toss in the trash?

Some do, others don't

Each industry has its own practice and philosophy about leaving messages. And I have my own style, too. Some colleagues tell me they won't leave messages on a cold call under any circumstance. I don't take that position. I think, why go through all the trouble of locating the prospect, preparing a warm-up, jotting down notes, setting the plan of action, working through anxiety, just to say, "Thank you very much," to a secretary or to hang up if I get an answering machine?

I like my time to pay off. It often does. After a week of prospecting and leaving messages, I usually receive calls from a handful of people.

On the flip side, around the telephone prospecting world, you'll run into two types of people—mayonnaise and Miracle Whip. Some people don't return calls and some do. (Some only return calls after receiving two or three messages.)

Think of it this way: If you don't leave a message, how is your prospect going to call you back?

How many times?

Basically, for every 3 to 4 numbers I dial, I speak to one person on my list. I probably leave messages more than twice as often as I talk to a prospect. How often should you call and leave a note for someone? Try calling once a day every few days, or weekly. Be wary of pestering your prospect and diluting your effectiveness. Give your prospect time to get back to you. She could genuinely be very busy, or out of town.

I have a colleague who sets a limit of leaving six messages. By the time her prospects return her call, they are usually apologetic for not calling sooner. And, from their embarrassment, they are often willing to offer her at least thirty minutes in a face-to-face meeting. For her, persistence pays off.

If you've left a couple of messages, but to no avail, keep trying.

Don't give up—you haven't had a chance to tell your story. Some days it seems people are poised at their desk just waiting for my call. At those times I prospect hard and strong.

Of course, the number of messages you leave and how far apart depends on how critical your situation is. If I'm facing a deadline, I'm relentless. Use common sense and instinct.

Meanwhile, she's at lunch

RRRing.

"She's not in right now. May I take a message?"

"Of course."

After you tap out the name and number routine, say something interesting and relevant. You want to grab the prospect's attention and call for action, so leave a clear but intriguing statement. Be courteous and make the message brief. But don't hang up yet. Start a conversation. Continue using language you feel comfortable with and words you believe in.

Always keep in mind that the people you reach have access to different types of information. I find most secretaries efficient and helpful—sure they'll stamp, mail, and fax to you and for you, but expect more. Secretaries are usually privy to people's schedules. They'll offer the names of other people you should call if your contact is busy or out of town. They're also familiar with people's work habits and who carries responsibility for which kinds of decisions in the organization.

A touch of goodwill

Trust the process and be willing to establish a commitment to yourself and your business. Believe me, persistence isn't a talent. It's a payoff for a little hard work and a dash of creativity.

And please, don't let people wear you down. I'll admit, though, one of the most difficult aspects of cold calling is being fresh and appealing every time out of the gate. But try. Make a deal with yourself and treat every call as though it were the most important conversation of the day. This deal is really important when you've had to leave messages.

TIPSTER

Already left three messages? Don't give up. Call again.

Your prospect will return from his lunch meeting full and relaxed only to be greeted with a stack of "while you were out" pink slips. You'll want him to notice your message. Use your positive energy and you'll consistently leave notes that people respond to. They'll be cold calling you!

Turn the tables

A few years ago, I had the good fortune to share some office space with a very successful salesperson. She could "telephone talk" more than anyone I knew. After leaving the details of her message, she'd keep talking. These two-way chats were strictly business related. At first, I thought her technique rather odd.

She'd never bully her way to the decision maker. She was crisp and polished with every message taker. And occasionally she'd greet a secretary who might say, "He wouldn't be interested." Or: "We really don't need that."

I listened to my colleague turn even those conversations around. She would remain pleasant and in an upbeat voice say:

"I didn't realize you made those kinds of decisions for the company. Tell me, how do you fit in? Sounds like perhaps we should meet."

I'm sorry, he's left the planet

Sigh. Don't you feel frustrated when your calls go unanswered? Here's what I do to reduce that tension. Usually on the third conversation with a secretary (I always write down his or her name in my notes) I'll say, "Ben, this is the third time we've talked. I had it in my notes he'd be out of the meeting by now, but he's not. I'm not in my office now, so when do you suggest I try again?"

Or, I might say "Is there someone else in the department you suggest I talk to?" To get a sense of each person's credibility or level of responsibility, I'm sure to ask each new contact a question.

"How do you fit in over there?"

"Do you know if anything is happening with the move out of state?"

"Would Martha Martinez be the best person to talk to?"

Usually I engage in these kinds of conversations after I've left my name, who I am, why I'm calling. Then I say, "You know, maybe you can help me. While I've got you on the phone, perhaps you can fill me in."

Honesty is the best policy

Some telephone prospectors use scare tactics when leaving messages. Beware. This approach can give birth to a shaky business relationship at best.

Imagine receiving this message, "It's about your children. Please give me a call, Sean Summerfield, 857-5209."

Be prepared for the consequences of using scare tactics. People are going to doubt what you have to say after you've left such a message. Picture their frame of mind by the time the parents call back.

"What about my kids?" says a frantic voice on the other end.

And you say, "Well, we've got this cute little playground we're installing in the neighborhood." By then, you've probably lost their interest, and the sale. I'm a fan of the direct, honest approach.

Many years ago a female colleague told me how she quickly reached top male management. When secretaries said, "May I tell him what this is regarding?" she'd say, "It's personal," suggesting that her call was very private (when it wasn't). Every time, she slid past gatekeepers. I always wondered what kind of business relationship she managed to build after using such a deception. I advise against using this tactic, too.

If you feel comfortable engaging in cryptic communication when leaving a message, that's okay, if it is honest.

☎ **"It's about the gas mileage in your car."**

☎ **"It's about the market value of your summer cottage."**

☎ **"It's about the food for your wedding."**

Trust yourself, and your product or service. You'll develop a distinctive style that will get your calls returned.

Your army of prospectors

recruit each secretary, administrative assistant, and work group colleague to be a part of my quest. You should do the same. After my introduction,

TIPSTER

Don't use scare tactics when leaving messages.

I explain my goal, and ask for the name of someone who can help me in the meantime. Always be on the look out for new names and more information to add to your prospect's profile. You'll be surprised how details and sales fall into place.

"Perhaps you can help me. I'm not completely sure if John Edwards is the person to work with me on this." This approach quickly warms up the conversation. If you are in the correct department, keep moving forward.

"What's his schedule look like?"

It's possible your contact keeps early or late hours. Find out.

"Gee, he must be very busy, when is a good time to call?"

Suppose you're promoting wrist pads recently invented for alleviating carpal tunnel pain. Talk to this new contact about symptoms. Express your genuine concern. Let him in on the importance of this issue. Then ask,

☎ **"Who else do you suggest I speak to?"**

☎ **"Who else is involved in that decision?"**

He may say, "Oh, Joan Leong delegates that to Peter Heffner."

Get the number, thank him very much, and place the next call. Now you have a warm-up for Peter Heffner.

Don't tell her I told you so

Suppose the person who gave you the name of a prospect requests anonymity. Or you got the name from people who are not at an equal level in the organization. What do you do?

☎ **"Hi there, I'm Bob Coates from Abbott Reality. Your name came up in conversation twice today. You may want to know about us. Do you have some time to talk now?"**

Your prospect may show some reserve.

☎ **"Who gave you my name?"**

In this case you might try this approach:

☎ **"Oh, I don't have those names in front of me, but your name has two checkmarks by it."**

☎ "I just got off the phone with John Edward's office, and they suggested I phone you. Can you spare a few moments?"

Hello, you rang?

Peter Heffner is not in, you leave a powerful message, and move on to the next call. Two hours later, your phone rings and it's a deep voice, "Peter Heffner here, returning your call." Fumble. Shuffle. Uhhhh. "Hi." "Who is Peter Heffner," says your left brain to your right brain. Hopefully you've been writing legible notes. Put Peter on hold after you say, "I need to change phones," and collect your thoughts. It isn't so rare that people call you back. Be prepared.

TIPSTER

I recruit each secretary and administrative assistant to take part in my quest.

We have the wrong suspect

Luckily, we don't need to talk to the president of every company. Ever waste days, even weeks, looking for a person and then in the end, learn he's the wrong guy? Be smart. Continually confirm that the person you're pursuing is indeed the one you need to reach.

☎ "I understand that Tomas Satelo plans special events for the bank. Is that correct?"

☎ "Is it true that he's the marketing director?"

☎ "I'm told she's in manufacturing. Exactly what does she do?"

☎ "Do you know of others that I should be talking to?"

☎ "I understand that Barbara Hunt makes the financial decision. Who does she rely on to review new programs?"

☎ "I don't have his title here, I know it has to do with human resources, can you help me out?"

☎ "Who else in the company does he talk to about . . . ?"

Answering machines and voicemail

The answering machine is a misnomer. It doesn't answer questions, nor does it offer much information. But with it, you can command a prospect's attention. Answering machines are the closest we get to a contact without talking directly to him or her. One advantage of the ubiquitous answering machine is that we have the luxury of leaving a longer message allowing you to be more expressive. Strengthen your voice message just by believing in who you are and how you sound. So go ahead and lay out your idea. And practice leaving warm-ups.

☎ **"I understand you'll be interested in this. John Levine suggested I phone you. Hope we can talk soon."**

☎ **"I really think this is something you might want to know about."**

Remember, too, that not everyone who has an answering machine or who is hooked into voicemail is happy about it. Some people feel harassed by technology. Just in case some of your prospects may be among this group, let them know you sympathize. Usually by the third voicemail message, I'll say, "I hope I'm not being bothersome." This is sometimes just the right nudge to get them to call me back.

Speak and spell

Once again, recall messages you respond to—and those you don't. When the answering machine beeps and the voice sounds confident, coherent, and professional, you probably reach for a pen and scribble down the name. How many times have you had to play back messages, just to get all of a telephone number, or to hear what someone was trying to tell you?

Speak slowly into machines and recite your telephone number twice. Unless your name is Mary or John Smith, spell it. Imagine the confusion when your prospect hears a muffled female voice on the answering machine, "Hi, this is Joe Banducchi." Speak slowly and clearly. "Hello, this is Joan Guiducci—G-u-i-d-u-c-c-i."

Let your personality brighten the black box on your contact's desk. Prospects will appreciate you and be motivated to return your call.

Try an alternate route

Are your voicemail messages being treated like junk mail—ignored? Don't persist in these cases. After three or four foiled efforts, go back into the switchboard or main number and ask to speak to someone in the department or in another area of the company.

TIPSTER

Speak slowly into machines and recite your telephone number twice.

☎ "I've been ringing Sara Chermack for a week now and haven't found her in. She must be very busy. Is it always like this for her?"

☎ "Is she out of the office?"

Explain why you're calling and ask:

☎ "Is Sara the person who can answer my question? . . . What would you suggest that I do?"

At this point, to whom are you talking? Does this voice belong to a receptionist, secretary, administrative assistant, or the person who sits at the desk next to your contact? The goal is to connect with someone who can help you reach the prospect or someone else who may be a more likely contact.

If you've reached a colleague, find out if she is involved with Sara's projects.

☎ "Do you work with Sara Chermack? . . . How do you fit in the organization?"

☎ "Are you involved in systems operations?"

If so, you may be rounding the corner, closer to home on the sale.

We need it yesterday

Believe me sometimes you need to speak to someone in a hurry. Once I had a contract nearly complete, but I needed paperwork from purchasing. My company had already guaranteed delivery. Gearing up for panic mode, I dialed the numbers.

"Perhaps you can help. There may be someone else in the group I can talk with. The pressure to meet a deadline will be nearly impossible if I don't get started on this today. Any suggestions?"

One time, my only option was leaving a voicemail message.

"Marketing is anxious to get this done. I understand you can help. We've got a deadline I hope we can meet."

When my job is to close the sale, I aim to keep the ball in my court. Rarely will I ever sit back and wait for the phone to ring. I make another call and go for results.

Telephone
Talk

When I sold office equipment for a living, I'd pack my car with machines, I'd collect money, do the installation—whatever it took to make the sale. I still refuse to wait for people to do things for me. Remember that intimacy with your product or service can make the difference between a sale and a loss. And if you can't install it yourself, make sure you know who can. Pronto!

My motto is: Take every opportunity and get the maximum mileage out of it. And move on to the next project.

Leaving voicemail messages—some examples

Be direct and straightforward. Remember keywords: short, clear, concise.

☎ "Hello, Jim. This is Jerry Jones with American Fidelity. I'm talking to Laura Summers about a pretty exciting program. Something new. She thinks that you might be interested as well. Hope to talk soon. You can reach me at . . . ."

☎ "Hello. This is Jeff Sanfruz. S-a-n-f-r-u-z. I'm with Big Time in Chicago. My toll free number is 800-555-1234. We have a program for new businesses like yours. Something I think you should know about. I'll try again tomorrow if I don't hear from you today. Again, my number is 800-555-1234."

☎ "Hello. This is Margaret Poe with The Grass Is Greener. I was driving through your neighborhood yesterday and noticed your house. The landscaping really stands out. I'm calling to talk to you about it. My number is 415/333-2189."

☎ "I think you'll be interested in knowing about this."

☎ "I understand there's been talk about changing office supply vendors. You would probably be interested in knowing about our special plan for new customers."

Use warm-ups with support staff

☎ "Bob Salamanca and I are talking about a new program. He thinks Susan Chen might be interested as well."

☎ "There's a new service he should know about. He may

have seen the article last week in the *Business Journal*."

☎ "I understand she's the office manager. We have a program that's working well for other law firms in town. I thought she would want to know about it. Do you know when she'll be out of that meeting?"

☎ "I know he'd want to take care of this."

☎ "I spoke to Nancy Lombardi in operations and she suggested I talk to him."

☎ "I didn't want to overlook anyone."

Be courteous. Spell your name before being asked. And give a time you'll be available if you're leaving your office.

☎ "I'm back in the office after 3 P.M."

Confirm the responsibilities of your contact

☎ "I understand she approves the advertising budget. Is that true? . . . How does she fit in? . . . What's her title? . . . What groups report to her?"

☎ "Perhaps you can help me. I'm calling about a sales training program. Is it true that he's involved in those decisions? . . . How does he fit in? . . . Who else is involved?"

☎ "I'm told Mary Lammers is the best person to start with about purchase orders for the South City office. Is that true? . . . Does she have an assistant or someone that may be able to answer a couple of questions?"

Facing a deadline? (talk to support staff)

☎ "I'm calling about a meeting next Thursday morning for controllers and other financial people. Do you know if his calendar is free? . . . Oh, I see. Perhaps there's a senior financial adviser in the group I should talk to about it. Who would that be?"

☎ "We have a meeting scheduled with engineering next Tuesday morning at ten o'clock that she may want to attend. Do you know if her calendar is free?"

TIPSTER
Remember
two key words:
Clear and concise.

☎ "Perhaps you can help me. I've been calling since last week. He must be very busy. I don't mean to be bothersome. I'm sure he'd like to know about our program. Perhaps there's someone in his group he relies on. To whom do you suggest I talk about . . . ?"

Find out prospect's schedule. Be sure to mention yours

Avoid leaving a message unless you can be reached. State a window of time you'll be available.

☎ "I'm in the office every day from 8 A.M. until noon."

☎ "You can always reach me after 4 P.M."

☎ "I'll hold. I'd like to talk with her if I can. Do you know how long she might be?"

☎ "When do you suggest I call her back?"

☎ "Do you know when he'll be out of that meeting? . . . How does his schedule look afterwards?"

☎ "Do you know her schedule for the rest of the day?"

☎ "How does his calendar look this week?"

☎ "How early does she start her day?"

☎ "How late does she stay at the office?"

☎ "I was hoping to reach him directly. I'm out of the office now and can't be reached. I left a message yesterday. How does his calendar look later today?"

☎ "Can I reach him at 989-0402 if I call after 5 P.M.? We're 2 hours behind in Phoenix and that might work better for me."

☎ "Does she have time first thing in the morning before she leaves for the office? . . . Would evenings be better? . . . The weekend?"

☎ "I wouldn't want to interfere with dinner. What would be the best time in the evenings to reach her?"

Practice professional courtesies

If you've left a message for Helen Midyett, and Steve Wood resolved your problem, call Helen back. Let her know your concerns have been addressed.

The wrap-up

Work to create interesting messages that leave your prospect curious about your call. But strive for clarity, and brevity. And always take the time to talk with message takers.

CHAPTER 6

6
For the record—keep notes, wisely

Data data everywhere

Early in my career you would have thought I thrived on chaos. My desk looked like a refrigerator door tacked with scribbled notes to myself and blurred memos on napkins. I reached for phone numbers, contract dates, and quotes on yellow Post-it™ notes.

Pretty naive, right? To think I could locate essential information during a call and sound sharp while shuffling paper napkins. I also believed I could recollect conversations, people's names, and titles as if they were colored with indelible marker on my memory.

That was until I heard my manager skillfully interweave bits of information into conversations that developed legs of their own, and actually went somewhere. He'd bring up a third party's opinion, past telephone conversations, articles he'd read. He spoke with authority and was very successful. I call it three-dimensional talk. I compared my cold calls,

which were flat and somewhat skeletal, at best, to his. Now, I had discovered another difference between an amateur and a professional. I realized that being able to recount events holds a lot of power.

People will listen and believe what you have to say. They'll know you've listened to them and remembered. Who isn't gratified when this happens to them?

Sales and the art of information maintenance

In recent years, a computer and a few pet software programs have streamlined my information retrieval and storage dilemma. With a flick of my fingers over a few command keys my client and prospect data base flashes on the screen in rows, columns, and—you got it—readable form.

I rarely miss a follow-up phone call, and I know what mail has been sent to whom. I still feel good every morning, setting my coffee cup next to a neat and solid list of people I should be sure to call.

This pet software I've mentioned is designed specifically for managing your contact list. Believe me, it makes everything so much easier. I know prospecting can by trying, that's why we need all the help we can get to help us iron out the wrinkles in the process. With my software and data base, I can produce analytical reports, select prospects living in the same zip code area, or list customers' purchases within the last 6 months, for example.

I don't limit my data gathering to just facts. I note the contact's mood, the weather, newspaper articles, mutual friends—anything to personalize the next call. With all of this literally at my fingertips, my clients and prospects know I'm right there with them (even though I try to be a few steps ahead).

It's possible you don't have a computer, but have access to one at the office. Here's a suggestion. Take advantage of computer access and put your contact list into a data base with all the particulars you need to start a direct-mail campaign, for instance. And continually update client contact and prospect files. A computer only reports back to you what you report to it.

These lists take years to build and are priceless to your business.

They also usually reflect your professional wealth. You can often spot a successful business by the depth of the contact list.

I knew a senior manager who was a real stickler for keeping the corporate mailing list updated and flawless. He was always cleaning up the data base and adding fresh names. In an industry where the direct mail response rate rests at 2 percent, his response rate reached 8 to 10 percent, every time.

Granted, not everyone uses a computer data base. Remember my manicurist? She keeps detailed, accurate, current data on index cards in a recipe box. She sees today's clients as avenues to tomorrow's business. During promotions, she'll walk her fingers through the alphabet, locating each customer's manicure-pedicure history. This simple system has encouraged her business to grow. She's so successful I now have to schedule appointments days in advance.

Don't let me mislead you. I am still the willing victim of original documents and papers and file folders. The computer has not replaced the four-drawer file cabinets, at least not for me. The myth of the paperless office is really just that—a myth.

But as I look around my office at the computer, fax machine, voicemail, and my fancy telephone complete with conference calling, speaker phone, and redial, I am reminded of the ease and speed of doing business in the 1990s. I suggest you treat yourself and invest in equipment that will simplify your business day. Although you'll probably still need a file cabinet!

A shopping list

There are many contact management software products to choose from and many features to look for. But the one you choose would allow you to:

- import mailing lists you purchased on disk into your data base.
- enter and retrieve records from your data base, easily.
- personalize the fields in your data base for each prospect or category of prospects.
- get help on-line through a function key.
- produce reports by alpha, date, or area code, and so on.

- produce customized reports.
- keep details of a conversation on a notepad utility.
- schedule appointments or follow up dates, and mailings on a calendar utility.
- gain access to a word processor to produce documents and letters.
- produce lists by separating the records you want from others in the data base.
- retrieve all records by geographic location, other common denominators.
- print labels and envelopes.
- learn to use it, with relative ease.
- get telephone support from the manufacturer.

Take a snapshot of the situation

Why is all of this organizing and note taking so important? Let me give you a clearer picture. I remember a sales month that was coming to a close. You're probably familiar with the pressure to meet forecasted numbers. Well, I had a $60,000 contract in progress. My contact, the senior manager at her company, gave me a verbal go-ahead. This agreement was reached during a series of telephone conversations, and you can believe I detailed every word and nuance in my notes.

My company needed a copy of the signed contract to complete the sale. On Monday, the week of month's end, I telephoned my contact, the senior manager, Diana Potts.

"Oh, she's in Palm Springs for 2 weeks, Joan," said the secretary. I froze. I turned to my computer screen for a picture of the situation. I asked the secretary if she could find the contract on Diana's desk. And she did.

"My notes say she has agreement from everyone," I said. "It seems all we need is the controller's signature. Do you know if Julian Brady is in the office?" She said he was. So I called him.

"Hi Julian, this is Joan Guiducci with North Bay Company. You may know of us. I've been working with Diana Potts for some time now on installing the network switch. Has she talked to you about the plans

Company: Series Research

Contact:	Potts		
Name:	Diana Potts	Last Call:	5/22
Company:	Series Research	Recall:	5/27
Address:	P.O. Box 196952	Title:	MIS Director
2nd Line:		Product:	N IV
City, State:	Los Angeles, CA		
Zip:	90021	Type:	Electronics
Workphone:	1-213-555-1234	Dear:	Diana
Fax Number:	1-213-555-2695	Other Contacts: 5M	

Notes

5/22 Ok by legal, re: terms and conditions. Schedule install and training asap. Will process paperwork by end of month.
5/17 Sent contract. Diana P. to review personally then forward to legal. expects quick turnaround. Technical review, flying colors. Julian Brady, Controller, signs contract.
5/1 Spoke to Carol Marks and Tim Sutton, answered questions. Reviewing technical documents. Expect to submit reccomendation within 2 weeks.
4/25 Demo-went well [concerns re: downtime durnig install], Great group.

to go ahead with the purchase?"

"Yes, I'm familiar with it."

"Great, I could use your help with the paperwork. Diana is out of town this week. She's reviewed our terms and conditions and finds them acceptable. Diana hoped we could process the order this week and plan for the installation. The only detail left is your signature. Her secretary can get the contract over to your office today. Is there any reason why you can't sign it by tomorrow and fax a copy to my office?"

"I don't see why not, I'll look out for it."

The contract was faxed to my desk within hours. The ending was a happy and profitable one. A $60,000 order was all the motivation I needed to create a sense of urgency. As it turned out, I didn't need Diana Potts to complete the transaction. My notes were accurate and detailed enough that I could sort out and solve the problem. That sale made my day, and my month.

Reaching the moment of truth

Once I spoke with a decision maker who played the "We're going to put the decision off" tune. My position was let's make a deal. Now. My notes paid off again.

"I don't think we should make any changes for at least 60 days," he said. "There's a risk the installation will interrupt production and cause a delay in our schedule. We can't afford that."

This was the moment of truth. I knew where I took the conversation next would tell the tale. There would be no second chance. If I'd listened to his tune this time, I'd never hear another.

"That's precisely the reason we should go ahead. And as quickly as possible," I said, and continued turning knowledge into wisdom. "I spoke to Jim Elliott just last week about this very issue. He believes he can cut design time by 30 percent or more if we go ahead now. We've also worked out an installation schedule. It should go something like this . . . ."

This technique of providing details that help the prospect see exactly how the product will benefit him or her moves any sales process forward. Allow yourself to use the data you've gathered, to push past any resistance, which is often just a concealed request for more information.

Another time a client referred a prospect to me, but not without a warning. I was told he was picky for details. I put this critical point in my prospect notes and then wooed him with facts and figures. We soon did business together.

Try to automate your contact list.

Here's some advice. Spend enough time preparing for and thinking through each call. And when the moment of truth arrives—and it will—you'll use information wisely. You'll be glad you did when you watch your business grow.

The amateur and the professional

Each time you speak to someone, you're building a history and will continue the story with the next call. Get details into the data base and use them next time out as warm-ups. People will be amazed with your memory.

☎ "Gee, the last time we spoke was in March and you were recovering from the tornado . . . ."

☎ "The last time we spoke, you were involved in the Baldini project."

This technique harks back to three-dimensional talk. Here's a portrait of an amateur, foolish enough to trust his memory.

The phone rings in the amateur's office.

"Hi, this is Bill Bates."

Silence. This amateur keeps sketchy notes on Post-it™ notes. He looks up and sees Bill Bates' name on the bulletin board, but nothing else. Only the name is written down. What kind of a reminder is that?

"Hello, Bill. How can I help you?" he asks. Our amateur would be able to help if he could remember exactly who Bill Bates is and what he needs. Eventually Bill reminds the amateur why he is calling—because the amateur's company called him months ago, and now he is ready to buy. Except now Bill is not too impressed with amateur's lack of quick wit and springy responses.

Let's rewind the video and push play. We can establish rapport immediately and professionally.

The phone rings.

"Hi, this is Bill Bates."

"Bill, good to hear from you. May I put you on hold for a moment while I change phones?" We flip to the B section in our data base and find Bates, Bill. That's right. He was the guy whose roof blew off during the tornado. The Bates' notes mention a follow-up date for October. It's September. Bill is on the ball, and so are you.

"Thanks for holding. Is it fall already? Seems like we just spoke a few weeks ago. Your renovations on the house must be nearly finished. By the way, Judy Merger is a steady customer now. I guess it's time we talk seriously, too."

You'll put people at ease by knowing what's going on and not expecting them to know it for you.

TIPSTER

Write your plan
in big letters
and tape it to the
wall in front of you.

Takes notes before you dial, too

Prospecting means you are calling "them" and that puts you in control. Always spend a few moments organizing. It's helpful to summarize any comments and questions on paper in front of you. Sometimes I tape my plan of action written in big letters—SET AN APPOINTMENT—to the wall. Review notes, plan your conversation and keep documents handy. Ask yourself what you need to know, and why. You may develop a list that includes these items:

- date
- key phrases
- issues to discuss
- questions to ask
- contacts or conversations that can be mentioned
- Who was my prospect?
- Where and when did this call occur?
- What did I say?
- What did my prospect say?
- How did we close?
- When will you talk again?
- follow up
- action
- referrals and their phone numbers

Practice warm-ups, use information, and sell

- Suppose you spoke to Janet Marks about your service, and she asked you to phone her again. So you do. Notice how deep and personal—three-dimensional—these following interactions are.

☎ "School's out next month. How are the plans going for your daughter's graduation? . . . You may want to know that houses in your neighborhood are selling very well right now. Are you and your husband moving up north this summer? . . . We should start making plans soon. How does your schedule look for later this week, say, Thursday or Friday?"

- Suppose you run a prenatal education center.

   ☎ **"Hi, Robert. Last time we spoke, you had just found out your wife was expecting. And now she's due in just 8 weeks. We should enroll you and the baby in classes now. Shall I sign you in for mornings or afternoons?"**

- Imagine you are phoning John MacIntyre, addressing some concerns he had. You might say the following:

   ☎ **"Last month you thought the reorganization might be in place by now. How's that going? . . . There are more options than I first thought. They look good. I think you'll be pleased. What we're able to do is this . . . . Have I overlooked anything? . . . The next thing we should do is sit down and look at the contract. How does your schedule look for next week?"**

- Finally, you locate another decision maker, and you are calling to include her in the discussion of your product.

   ☎ **"Doug Conway and I are talking about a new manufacturing process that can cut costs by 30 percent or more. He isn't sure about the contract with your current supplier. He thought you could fill me in."**

- Let's say you're working with one department in a company and you've got a lead on another project elsewhere in the organization.

   ☎ **"I'm working with Barbara Cole organizing her sales meeting in Chicago next month. She tells me that you're responsible for the user's group meeting. I may be able to help. Have you set a date yet?"**

A detailed track record

Here's more advice. Take a time-out after each call to summarize and collect your thoughts, then write them down. Also review your performance. How could you have improved that last call?

Follow through on your plan of action; that is, call when you promise to and drop the packages in the mail at the appointed times. Mark dates on calenders. Get new contacts onto the appropriate list. Add to your master list. Make up mailing labels or envelopes for new prospects.

How you keep records is, in the end, your decision. Choose from index cards, file folders, or computer programs. Whatever you do, choose a system that will grow with your business. If you try to keep all the details in your head, you'll lose your prospects, your clients, and your mind.

Just do it

Keeping records of telephone prospecting, for me, is as routine as visiting the salad bar at noon, everyday.

I keep at least three types of records: daily, weekly, and prospect data sheets. This last record helps to qualify my leads. I include the following kinds of information in my records.

- Is this prospect interested in a future conversation?
- Did we develop a rapport?
- Is this person enthusiastic about my product or service?
- What questions did she ask?
- What comments did he make?
- What objections did she state?
- Who else is involved, and how?

Always remember to tally messages left and busy signals met. If you are exclusively a telemarketer, you're probably expected to account for your calls on a daily and weekly basis. If you are your own boss, build this discipline into your schedule. Why? Because this sort of record helps you see progress and recognize that production drops when you slack off. Lick and stick a star next to sales, requests for orders, and goals achieved.

Golden selling hours

Devise a time management schedule. I devote certain hours to pros-

TIPSTER

Note details into your files and use them as warm-ups for your next call.

pecting only. I've come to value that time, and you should too. It is crucial to your growth. Try asking friends and family not to call during those hours. They'll respect your requests.

Keep people's work habits in mind, and remember the varying time zones across the country. I've found my golden selling hours: between 8 A.M. and 10 a.m., and between 2 P.M. and 4 P.M. I've also found that many executives working late tend to be receptive (after secretaries have left for the day).

Perhaps you already consider your golden selling hours to be between 6:30 and 8:30 in the evening, at people's homes. If so, you might also try phoning them during the day. It seems that more people are working from home, so you might capitalize on that trend.

The wrap-up

Please keep notes because you can't store everything neatly in your brain. Recordkeeping is critical to your success. Set goals for yourself. Determine how fast you want to outgrow your office space. And break the numbers into monthly, weekly, daily, even hourly objectives. Keep asking yourself how many and what type of new clients do you want.

Keep track of your progress. How many calls are you making every day?

How much time do you spend telephone prospecting? How long is each call? You probably are paid according to results, not hours spent, or wasted.

Count the calls per day you make. How many stories did you tell? Keep a list of successful connections. These are the telephone calls that result in a conversation with the prospect's name on your list.

Not only is keeping records logical, it shows you where you've been, and where you're going. Ahhh. Direction. By each week's end, you can congratulate yourself or kick yourself, gently.

TIPSTER

Devote certain
hours in your week
to prospecting only.

Power Calling™ Daily Call Report

Name: _____   Date _____   Day: S M T W T F S

Contact/Company	Action									New Contact.			Notes
	CC	LM	MC	Appt	Lit	FU Call	Cont. Sign	Other		Ref	B Grp		
							$						
							$						
							$						
							$						
							$						
							$						
							$						
Totals							$						

CC = Cold Call   FU Call = Follow up call (Date=e.g. 10/1)
LM = Left Message   Cont. Sig=Contract signed ($10,000)
MC = Made Contact   Ref= Referral
Appt= Appointment Made (Date=e.g. 10/1)   B. Grp= Buying Group
Lit = Sent literature (F=Fax, M=Mail)

Power Calling™ Weekly Wrap Up

Name: _____

Week Ending: _____

	New Contact		Action								
	B Grp	Ref	Other	Cont. Sign	FU Call	Lit	Appt	MC	LM	CC	
Sunday				$							
Monday				$							
Tuesday				$							
Wednesday				$							
Thursday				$							
Friday				$							
Saturday				$							
Totals				$							

CC = Cold Call
LM = Left Message
MC = Made Contact
Appt = Appointment Made
Lit = Sent literature

FU Call = Follow up call
Cont. Sig = Contract signed
Ref = Referral
B. Grp = Buying Group

CHAPTER 7

7
Qualities of a professional— you have them

What does that "p" word mean?

Through the years, I've been defining my idea of professionalism. I've decided that professionalism is a combination of things, but the most important element is attitude. If Merriam Webster were to ask me, for my definition of professional, I'd say, "Being a professional is knowing that what you do is important, and that you recognize that doing it to the best of your ability is essential." People who care about their work, and take pride in their work, strive for total quality.

Professionals are reliable; you can trust them to fulfill their promises. For example, I act quickly to put literature in the mail, to follow up on the set time, and am never late for appointments. I respect people's time, and they appreciate that. Hold your head high and take responsibility for the services you provide, or fail to provide.

People pay professionals for their service, expertise, and

TIPSTER

Work hard
to build and
maintain unique
business
relationships.

knowledge—and will pay for these again and again. This means professionals work hard to build and maintain unique business relationships. Closing the big sale, moving on, never contacting the buyer again, is for beginners and amateurs only.

Telephone prospecting, we both know, can be tedious and sometimes deflating to the old self-esteem. When I feel this happening I confirm my ideals of professionalism and feel confident that what I am doing is important. I am doing the best job I can. As soon as you see the results of your efforts, and you will, the tedium will dissipate and you'll feel more relaxed and confident. In this chapter I've presented a few more things I've learned along the way about being a professional.

Not in the pages of Vanity Fair

A professional has style. But style is not conferred by donning silk blouses or beautiful ties. Nor is it defined by the car you drive. Style is substance. It's what you say and how you say it. Think sincerity and authority.

I believe style is how far you will go to fulfill the needs of prospects, colleagues, clients, and customers. Help those you meet along the way. When I look for chances to fulfill other's dreams and desires, I am enhancing my own. Being professional means being human, so understand and work to please clients. They'll come back to you for more business. Wouldn't you?

Your voice, yourself

By now you've cultivated your market. You've targeted correctly. No longer are you attacking the white pages of the telephone book. Now, how do you sound?. Have you truly considered your tone of voice, and the pacing of words and phrases? Do you hear a friendly lilt? Are you pausing here and speeding up there? Is every word audible, casual, inviting? Prospects only see what they hear and that first impression is a lasting impression. A smile in your voice works in mysterious ways.

Prospecting style

The best way to develop a successful telephone talk is, as we suggested before, placing yourself on the other end of the call. The phone rings, intruding into the silence, interrupting your project, disturbing your reading, and generally disrupting your concentration.

You answer and, immediately, you realize it's a cold call. How? Why do you hang up?

Perhaps this time, you listen to what the cold caller has to say. Why do you hang on?

I suggest keying into those elements snagging your attention. Is it the voice or the words used? Is this a personality, a likeable human being somehow coming through the telephone line to you? Really concentrate and answer these questions for yourself, and soon you'll develop a style that works for you.

TIPSTER

Telephone prospects only see what they hear. A smile in your voice works in mysterious ways.

Do re mi fa so la la la

What first meets the prospect's ear? His telephone receiver, and your voice. Both can be cold, hard, and plastic.

Immediately, you want to soften this less than perfect introduction. You can't squeeze your fingers through the telephone wire for a handshake, nor are we using technology to establish friendly eye contact. Your voice is your asset. Use it to shake hands and establish rapport.

Telephone Talk

I'm sure you've listened to yourself on an answering machine, or on a tape and said, "I sound like that?" The reproduction you hear is most likely closer to the real sound because we hear our own voice through our head. And that sound is distorted.

If you're like many people, you slur syllables together or garble letters and mumble words. It's a common malady. We're lazy talkers.

Try to listen for words with endings snipped off. Some of us tend to lose k's and g's and r's. Do you say ta for to instead of tu? Or wanna for want to? Customah? Without realizing it, many of us sound like this:

"We're goin' ta sendit ta ya."

Now let's spend some time here. Be objective and fair to yourself. Try taping your speech. As you replay it, your less than perfect words will be magnified. And lazy or sloppy speech habits are relatively easy to

TIPSTER
Record your
voice and improve
your sound.

remedy. Just pay attention to how you annunciate.

Remember, you have muscles around your mouth and jaw. Use them. Open your lips and work your jaw. Limber up. Then speak slowly. Soon, your sentences will become clearer. Give your words time to sink in.

Here's another tactic. Tune in to your conversations. By listening to your prospect's speech, you can mirror it. When he speaks slowly, you'll speak slowly. Reflect some of the words she uses.

Also listen to your lines of questioning. After you ask a question, close your mouth and let the prospect answer. We're so fearful of telephone silence. Do you ask questions, and keep talking? Work at creating a quiet self-confidence. Let there be calm moments in the presentation.

Being aware of your speech patterns and getting into the right rhythm move a conversation forward. Experiment with this approach and see where your words take you.

Pace, pause, and muse

Regardless of where you are in your career, you're probably prospecting for new business. On my first sales job I shared an office with an extraordinary salesperson. He was the number-one producer in the office.

I still remember how he spoke. It wasn't radio announcer quality, and was actually rather ordinary. But when he talked, people listened. He told me he was always working on how he sounded by talking into a tape recorder to stay sharp.

His pauses were strategically placed. Whenever he was asked a question or expected to make a point, he would always take a luxurious 4 to 5 second pause before responding. The effect on the listener was to settle down and listen.

I have also noticed that sentences ending with an upward or rising inflection invite a response. You sound spirited. And keeping your spirits up will encourage prospects to have a positive attitude to your call, and your product or service. And that helps close the sale.

As you walk your talk, mark up your script for speed, softness, loudness, and pauses. Just as a musician takes breaths, so must you. You're interpreting a score, too. So practice, practice, practice.

You better believe it

Testing your story and honing your script is like redecorating a home—you rearrange the furniture, add artwork to the walls, or buy a new fruit bowl. The results are a refreshing change of scenery. I like to extend this freshness to my prospects when I call.

To make pleasant, effective calls, consistently, you must believe in yourself and your product. Before you pick up the receiver, soothe the butterflies floating in your midsection. You know this person wants to hear what you have to say. Soon enough, you'll notice, as you sit up and talk straight, your prospect will sit up and take you seriously.

We've all heard that familiar axiom. Self-doubts breed product doubt from the prospect. The more confidence you exude, the more others will listen. It's true.

No substitute for knowledge

Learning to speak with authority means learning to spot trends in the news, and patterns in the economy. Stay abreast of who's who in your field and of what's going on.

After all sales is motivation. You motivate yourself to make the calls. And your conversation motivates the prospect to do something: listen, talk, negotiate, buy, whatever.

Here's another sales axiom. Know your product and know your story. Sharpen your presentation, so you can recite it with the same confidence you have when you count up to ten and down from ten (and from the middle, too).

Spontaneous delivery brings your product to life. Although you've presented it before, make the story seem as though you've just had the thought. Occasionally, change the order of your presentation. Try another sentence. Ask different questions.

TIPSTER

Add spirit to your words. Enthusiasm is contagious.

Relax and try some humor

Add a spirited quality to your words. Enthusiasm is contagious. You know as well as I do, people who plod along are boring. Prospects will say, "It rang, I answered, I listened, I snoozed." View each call as though it is the first of the day.

Laughter is a universal experience. I like to sprinkle wit and humor whenever I can as long as it rings true to the conversation. And yes, especially with a prospect I've just met. Laughter is a great icebreaker.

If I say something funny, I don't wait self-consciously for my prospect to laugh, I laugh first. But let me interject a word of caution here—moderation. Unless your dream is to make people laugh (in which case you belong in show business and not sales), telling jokes to someone you don't know is taboo and a bore.

Sounding lively and excited is enough. To get animated, picture colors. Your mind will shift and take on new energy. Now pump that energy into your call. You'll be amazed. Nurture that one spark and carry it through your next 10 calls.

It's not a crapshoot

One of the most difficult aspects of cold calling is allowing your best self to shine through to each prospect. Keeping fresh through the thirtieth call of the day is tough, but essential. Cold calling is not a crapshoot and you must avoid that mind-set.

One way to stay fresh is to believe that with this one call, you'll make the sale. I concede that making connections is a numbers game. For every three or four calls, you'll only reach one contact. And suddenly you're called upon to tell your story. What happens? If you're in a crapshoot mode, you're likely to be unprepared, blow the sale, and wade miserably through the next three or four phone calls.

Rather than believing in the crapshoot, a stockbroker I know decided to believe he would connect with every number he dialed. Since he's adopted this philosophy, he speaks directly to more decision makers. He also sets a time to cold call—9 A.M. to 11 A.M. This way, he doesn't face hours of calls. And he may complete his goal within 30 minutes. If

TIPSTER
Believe that every number you dial will be profitable.

so, he stops and pats himself on the back for a day well done.

His advice is, "Quit while you're ahead, on a positive series of calls. Why wait until your luck runs, excuse the pun, cold? Save your hot streak for tomorrow." He stops while he is hot, and faces the next session with a continuing passion for success.

Some like it hot

Still, everyone has his or her own method. I experience some days when words slip into place and conversations click into action. I take advantage of those times and make all the calls I've been putting off (yes, it happens to me too). When I'm hot, I keep going. You might consider experimenting and stay with what works best for maintaining a positive attitude.

Name disorder

Somewhere in the history of sales books we were told to say the prospect's name, so as to personalize, to get attention, to direct conversation. Well, we're all on to that game. And it's become a bit transparent. When you use someone's name over and over in the conversation, you may end up being perceived as obnoxious. Once or twice is okay, otherwise, the prospect will think you have a name disorder.

Sales don't stop there

Soothe and always congratulate your new clients and customers on making a good decision. They suffer what is called buyer's uncertainty. We've all have had that experience. After we have bought and paid for something, we look for ways to justify the purchase. Help your clients overcome their uncertainties once the sale is concluded. Send a new client a letter saying you are pleased about working with her now and in the future.

TIPSTER
Be there
for clients and
customers.

TIPSTER
Don't run
away from bad
news.

Reach out and touch

Always be there for your customers and clients. And be aware of what they need before they need it. Keep looking and sure enough, you'll find valid reasons to call them:

☎ "I've been studying your account and came up with a couple of ideas for improvement."

☎ "I'd like your opinion . . . ."

☎ "The company is thinking about promoting a new program, and we'd like your reaction . . . ."

If your prospect has posed a valid objection or concern during your initial approach, get in touch with her in a few months.

☎ "We've had a change in our program you should know about."

☎ "I have an article from the *Business Journal* you may want to see."

☎ "We haven't spoken since last September. I think you should know about recent developments with . . . ."

Now a a few words of caution. Keeping in touch doesn't mean pestering. Your calls must be legitimate and professional.

No news is not good news

Another key issue is that professionals don't run away from bad news. Withholding information can lose you a client, fast. You want credibility and appreciation. Be open and honest with clients. When you are, even when the news is not so great, a funny thing happens—the client remains loyal.

Surely you've encountered the dissatisfied customer. For you, being right is not the issue—it's how the customer feels after he hangs up the phone. Calm him down with understanding.

☎ "I understand you're disappointed. I'd like to resolve this, too. Tell me about the situation."

Express your regrets for what went wrong and be genuinely concerned about finding a solution. Let clients know you care. If they don't have to fight you, they'll help you reach an agreement. Gather all the facts.

TIPSTER

Put aside calls going nowhere.

Listen carefully to the who's, what's, where's, when's, why's, and how's. Take the client by the hand and relax. Take notes and attend to the matter, quickly.

The wrap-up

Professionals:
- always prospect for new business.
- believe the prospect will want to hear what they have to say.
- know their product or services and where they fit in the marketplace.
- have a story to tell.
- keep up with their own industry issues and trends.
- always introduce themselves first.
- are persistent—professionals call 3 or 4 times and succeed after the amateur has given up.
- ask for some time to talk.
- have a fresh, spontaneous, and genuine appeal, with every call.
- don't overwhelm prospects with too much detail and every buying benefit.
- won't make any claims they can't substantiate.
- engage in conversation, not monologue.
- limit interruptions (turn off call waiting).
- ask questions to steer the conversation.
- don't answer their own questions.
- promote a sense of urgency, move the sales process along.
- break ice with natural humor.
- are eager to improve cold-calling techniques.
- never sit and wait for life to happen.
- express themselves with conviction.
- seriously consider what a prospect thinks and feels.
- treat everyone with respect.
- keep prospect lists updated and flawless.
- keep accurate records
- review cold-calling performance (practice, practice, practice).
- fulfill promises.

- match solutions to needs.
- speak to each "spoke" in a buying group.
- confirm the responsibilities of contacts.
- stay in touch with prospects and clients.
- don't waste time with calls that are going nowhere.
- build business relationships, not just closes sales.
- strive for total quality.

Until next time

See yourself as a successful, professional salesperson and others will "hear" your view. If you are just starting out, dream a little bit. Visions certainly can't hurt, and they can be attained through hard work and persistence. Charm helps, too. Cultivate your natural charm. Any phony attempt is sure to be seen through. Enthusiasm is contagious. Laughter is infectious.

People want their day brightened, and you can do that for them. Just talk to people. See if you have what they need. Honor your luck and embrace serendipity. And when you succeed (and you will), you'll have earned it.

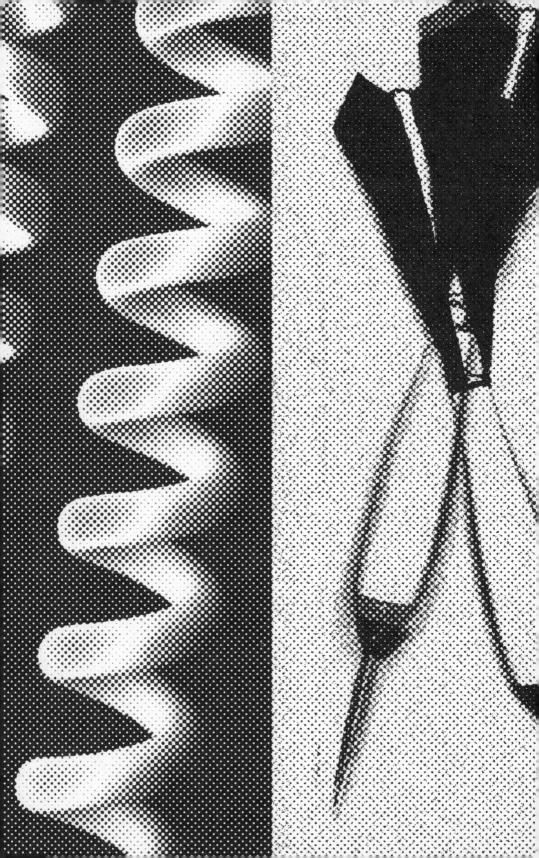

A cold caller's conversation

Suppose you own a specialized employment agency. Today you'll be prospecting to the managers of manufacturing companies. Your goal is to introduce yourself, determine the need for temporary or permanent employees, get information in the mail or over the fax, and set-up a follow-up appointment.

Rrring...

Prospect: Art Bromberg. (Note that he answers his own phone, and his voice sounds gruff.)

You: Hello, Art? This is Mary Butler from TechTemp Professionals.

Prospect: What is it?

You: Is this a bad time?

Prospect: I'm going to a meeting. What's this all about?

You: I understand you're involved in hiring engineers. That's why I'm calling. But we can talk another time. Is this afternoon better?

Prospect: I'm shorthanded this week. (Note this in his file, too.)

You: Would next week work for you?

Prospect: Not Monday. We have staff meetings all day.

You: Why don't I call on Tuesday?

Prospect: Well, you can try.

You: I'll call then. Thank you.

Although your prospect was abrupt, and sounded hurried, you weren't discouraged. In fact, you learned he's shorthanded—he demonstrated a strong need for your service. Remember to integrate this into your story when you call back.

Now suppose he had said, "Just put information in the mail."

You might have responded, "I won't really know what to send to you until we talk more."

Anyway, always keep your word and follow through. Call back on Tuesday.

You: Hello, Art. This is Mary Butler from TechTemp Professionals. We agreed to speak today. Is this a good time to talk, for 2 minutes?

Prospect: No time is really good. But tell me what you've got.

You: At TechTemp we specialize in placing technical people. I'm calling about some relief for you and your staff. I understand you're shorthanded on engineers—you mentioned this last week. I'm sure we can help. We can offer part-time help for you right away. Have you considered contractors for these peak times?

Prospect: We've thought about contractors. But we're concerned about the expense.

You: (Shift your approach.) We can also help with permanent placements. And there are several ways we can look at costs.

(Enter a third-party opinion.) You may know of us from our work with Phillips Industries down the street from your building. We have engineers assigned to them on temporary contract. Phillips was behind schedule on a critical program. They needed a way to catch up to meet a deadline. They're back on track now, and they've found that the contracting paid for itself. (Now ask questions.) Are you meeting schedules with your projects?

Prospect: We're behind on one. And a couple of new ones are closing in that we aren't sure how we'll staff.

You: Are these projects from your budget?

Prospect: Seems like they're always my budget. (He's warming up now.)

You: I'd like to fax you some detailed information for us to talk about. It's only two pages but full of valuable ideas and options. Think you might review them by this afternoon?

Prospect: It's possible.

You: Why don't we set a telephone appointment for tomorrow morning.

Prospect: Okay. Try me about eleven o'clock.

You: We have other technical people, programmers, technical writers, manufacturing specialists. Who else in your firm do you suggest I talk to?

Prospect: You might try Sharon Fransch in manufacturing.

You: Could you spell that for me?

Prospect: F-R-A-N-S-C-H
You: Is her number handy?
Prospect: She's on extension 2384
You: Thank you Art. The information is on the way. And I'll talk with you tomorrow morning. Good-bye.

Your very next call is to Sharon Fransch. Warm up that call by mentioning your conversations with Art in Engineering. Good luck!

By the way

Throughout my book, I've suggested you ask for names of contacts and referrals before hanging up the telephone. I'm going to follow my advice. Before you close the cover of *Power Calling*, think of a few friends who would benefit from what you've just learned. (Don't make the mistake of giving your book away —you'll refer to it again and again.) If *Power Calling* works for you, reach out and tell someone. It's your thoughtful way of wishing your colleagues success. And that reflects on you.

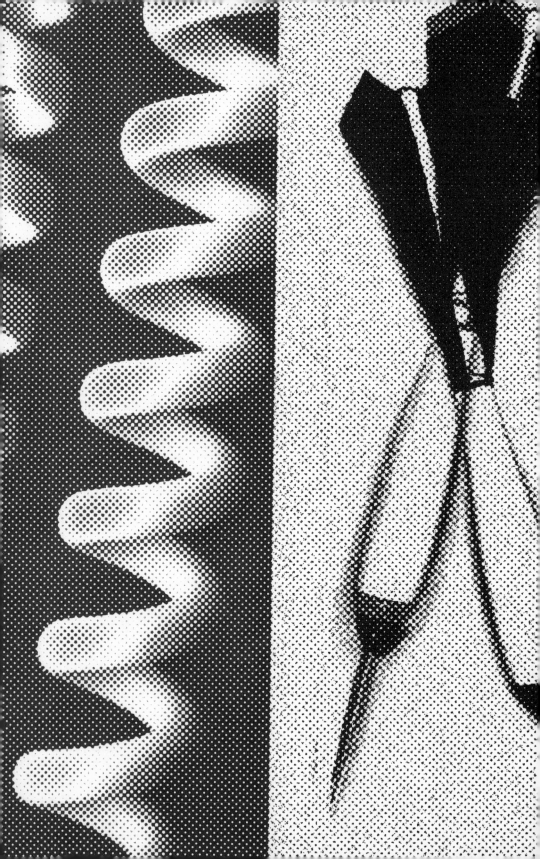

Sample Dialogue

Your accomplishments

"You may know us from the work we did for . . . ."

"We're one the best in the area at what we do . . . ."

"If you know . . . then you probably know of our work."

"We were the recipient of an award from our work with . . . ."

Public opinion

"The Chamber of Commerce published a survey placing us as one of the top five companies in town for customer satisfaction."

"The International Association of Stamp Collectors has endorsed our 12 color fax machine because they solve the problem of transmitting subtle colors and designs. We believe we can show you similar results. What are you using now?"

A third-party opinion

"Our clients are telling us how much money they're saving on this new program."

"I'm calling about an innovative program we've designed for small business owners like you. Our clients are telling use how much time they're saving."

"Bob Summers and I are talking about a new program. He thinks you may be interested as well."

"You may know of us through our association with Mid West Bank."

"Your neighbor, Jose Mandetta, is getting great results. It occurred to me that you'd want to be involved in this."

"John Yee suggested I speak to you, so I called right away. I don't want to overlook anyone."

A newspaper article

"I noticed the article about your company in yesterday's Journal. It occurred to me that you may be interested in our services."

"I understand that you saw the article in the City Journal. I've been talk-

ing to a lot of people about it for the last week. What's your interest in the
. . . ."

"I'm sure you read about us in the *Rochester Daily* business section."

Similar lifestyle

"We live in the same neighborhood."

"We belong to the same club."

"We know the same people."

"We closed the sale on a house right down the block from you. They're quite pleased with the offer. We still have a list of buyers interested in owning homes in your neighborhood. I think we should talk . . . ."

Common denominator

"We have a special promotion through the end of this month. Big savings for you. We're getting a strong response from other hospitals in the area. I thought you would want to know about it, too."

"We have a program that's being warmly received in the legal community. We've signed up several law firms in your part of town. I didn't want to overlook anyone."

Growing or fading trends

"You may have seen the recent news in the press about carpal tunnel syndrome. Doctors say anyone who types for more that 4 hours daily can be affected."

"We understand these volatile economic times, but people love to feel healthy. That's why we offer club memberships to fit every budget—from $200 to $ 2,000."

A simple observation or knowledge you have

"I was driving through the neighborhood yesterday and noticed your house. The landscape really stands out."

"I've been watching your company grow for the last few years. My background may be of some interest to you."

"I have some fresh design ideas for you. I am confident I can make your direct mail more effective. How are you producing your newsletters? . . . I think we should meet."

"I was in your store yesterday. You've done a great job remodeling the interior. What are your plans for the outside? . . . I know some changes would increase foot traffic—I nearly passed by your shop, so that means others must, too. I'll be downtown tomorrow, I'd like to drop by and show you some of my ideas."

"I understand your son is going off to college this fall. You may want to know about the recent increase of interested buyers in your neighborhood."

"I've studied your account and I have some ideas that can save you money."

"We've conducted a market analysis in your neighborhood. You may be amazed by the results. I'm able to get you a complimentary copy of the study. When was the last time you spoke to someone about the value of your home?"

"I'm in your part of town every week visiting my clients. I'd like to stop in and introduce myself."

Follow up on a direct mailer, or from a convention meeting

"There was so much excitement at the seminar, I'd like to speak to you now, while it's quiet."

"We spoke at the trade show about writing your practice newsletter. This type of quarterly contact shows your patients you care, keeps them informed on the latest in cosmetic dentistry, and keeps your patient base healthy."

"I'm following up on information I sent to you last week. Has it come across your desk? . . . I'd like to point out a couple issues."

"I stopped by your office the other day. You were busy in a meeting. I left some information. Have you had time to read it? . . . I'd like to point out a couple of items you might be interested in."

Product claim

"We've taken a unique approach to alarm systems. It's the future. Others in your neighborhood are installing now, saving money while they build their homes."

"We've developed that latest technology for firms in your field. You may be spending a lot of dollars unnecessarily—we can help you save money. How are you tracking your orders?"

"I'm calling about the health of you and your patients. What do you do with your instruments after they've been used? . . . We are introducing a sterilization process, we think you should know about."

"I understand that you're involved in manufacturing. We have a productivity tool that can shorten production time by at least 60%."

Virtues of your business and who you are

"I'd like to tell you a bit about who we are and what we do."

"We're big on quality, reasonable on cost."

"Since we don't know each other, I'd like to tell you about myself and the kind of work I do."

"I specialize in providing catering services for small business owners. I have spend the last 5 years working with . . . ."

"I'm good at developing other people's ideas into a tangible product."

"You may know of us from the district. We've been in the Haverfeld building for over 10 years now. It's been a long time since we talked to you. A lot has happened in the last few years that you may want to know about."

"I'm schooled in the latest technology, where others may be using outdated, old-fashioned methods to achieve similar results. I can save you money."

"I may be young and new to the area, but I assure you I have fresh ideas, a different perspective than people of a different generation."

Courtesies

"I didn't want to overlook anyone."

"I think you'll be interested in knowing about this."

"I wanted to personally talk to you."

"A neighbor is getting great results. It occurred to me that you'd want to get involved."

"I've heard your name mentioned a few times today."

Confirm the contact's responsibility

"I understand that you purchase office supplies for the company. Is that correct?"

"I understand that you're involved in managing the administrative side of the business. Is that correct?"

"I understand that you manage the shipping department?"

"I understand she's the office manager. We have a program that's working well for other law firms in town."

"I understand she approves the advertising budget. Is that true? . . . How does she fit in? . . . What's her title? . . . What groups report to her?"

Prospect is distracted

"It's best we talk when you have more time. I have an idea you might want to know about. I didn't want to overlook anyone. How does your schedule look this afternoon?"

"Sounds like you've got a few distraction now, perhaps I'll call back this afternoon. How does three o'clock look?"

"I wouldn't know what information to send until we talk more. How does your schedule look at . . . ?"

Qualify need and interest

"Tell me about . . . ."

"Did you read . . . ?"

"How long has it been . . . ?"

"When was the last time you talked to someone about . . . ?"

"What is your opinion?"

"What are your thoughts?"

"How many . . . ?"

"Would you explain . . . ?"

"What are your plans . . . ?"

"What are you doing about . . . ?"

"How have you approached the problem of . . . ?"

"Have there been discussions about . . . ?"

"How would you describe the way you're doing . . . ?"

"Have you considered . . . ?"

"Have you given thought to . . . ?"

"When do you think this will change?"

"How much have you budgeted for this? . . . Are those fund available now?"

"What cost would you be comfortable with?"

"When do you expect to add this to your budget?"

"Do you have the money in your budget?"

"Are you interested in this?"

Closes

"I think we have a fit here, we should talk more. How does your schedule look on . . . ?"

"I'd like to fax you some information we can talk about. It's only two pages, but full of valuable ideas and options for you. Do you think you might review them by Thursday? . . . . Let's set a telephone date for 2 P.M."

"I'll be in your neighborhood next Wednesday. I'm sure I can show you a way to cut back significantly on your expenses. How does your schedule look?"

"I don't think this is right for you at the moment. When do you see your situation changing?"

"I think I may have something for you, but I need to do some research. I'll be back in touch next Wednesday with that information. How does you calender look?"

"I'll put our catalogue in the mail and check with you from time to time."

"I'll pencil you in on the seminar schedule and get that fax to you now. Tomorrow I'll call to confirm and to sign up anyone else who might be interested."

"So, I'll see you Saturday at 10 A.M. And you have my number in case something comes up in the meantime."

Ask for referrals

"Do you have any projects coming up that I may be of help with? Or do you know of anyone who needs my services?"

"This may not be a fit here, but you probably know . . . ."

"You probably know a lot of people in the business. They may want to know about this new technology, too. Anyone come to mind that I could call on?"

"I understand that you know people in the association? They'll probably want an invitation, too. Any suggestions?"

"We also have a program that works well for young children. The money is set aside for their college fund. Anyone you can think of that should know about it?"

"Does each division have its own sales department? . . . Do they operate independently of each other? . . . Do you ever talk to one another? . . . Where do you suggest I start?"

"These new programs for small business owners. Any one from the Chamber of Commerce come to mind? . . . We'll need to act quickly. The company will waive the one-time, set-up fee only through the end of the month while we kick off this promotion."

Locate everyone in the buying group

"I'm talking to Bert Adams about engineering reports and Cheryl Brigham in finance. Have I overlooked anyone?"

"Do you know of others that I should be talking to? . . . I wouldn't want to overlook anyone."

"It occurred to me that manufacturing should hear about our plan. Where do you suggest I start?"

"I understand Barbara Hunt makes the financial decisions. Whom does she rely on to review programs?"

"I should talk to someone in the purchasing department about how to handle the paperwork. Where do you suggest I start?"

"Who else in the company does he talk to about these matters?"

Conduct a survey or interview

"We're interested in your reaction to . . . ."

"When is the last time you spoke to someone about your system?"

"Describe your approach to . . . ."

"How are you doing that now?"

"Anything you'd like to change?"

"Tell me about your current system?"

"Have you considered . . . ?"

"Who would be the best person for me to start talking with? . . . And how does she fit in?"

"Perhaps you can help me locate someone in the department. We have a system that . . . ."

Facing a deadline

"I'm having trouble getting through to Mark Wright. He's working on a deadline now. Any suggestions on someone else I could start with?"

"Perhaps you can help me. I've been calling Jane Runak since last week. She must be very busy. We're organizing a presentation. I'm sure she'd like to know about it. Perhaps we can include someone else from the group. What do you suggest I do?"

"I'm calling about a meeting next Thursday morning for controllers and other financial people. Do you know if his calendar is free? . . . Oh, I see. Perhaps there's a senior financial adviser in the group I should talk to about it. Who would that be?"

"We have a meeting scheduled with engineering next tuesday morning at ten o'clock that he may want to attend. Do you know if his calendar is free?"

Voicemail messages

"It's about the gas mileage in your car."

"It's about the market value of your summer cottage."

"It's about the food for your wedding."

"This is Jerry Jones with American Fidelity. I'm talking to Laura Summers about a pretty exciting program. Something new. She thinks that you might be interested as well. Hope to talk soon. You can reach me at . . . ."

"This is Jeff Sanfruz. S-a-n-f-r-u-z. I'm with Big Time in Chicago. My toll free number is 800-555-1234. We have a program for new businesses like yours. Something I think you should know about. I'll try again tomorrow if I don't hear from you today. Again, my number is 800-555-1234."

"I think you'll be interested in knowing about this."

"I understand there's talk about changing office supply vendors. You would probably be interested in knowing about our special plan for new customers."

Mention your schedule

"I'm in the office every day until noon."

"You can always reach me after 4 P.M."

Find out prospect's schedule

"Do you know when he'll be out of that meeting? . . . How does his schedule look afterwards?"

"How does her schedule look this week?"

"How early does she start her day?"

"I wouldn't want to interfere with dinner. What would be the best time in the evenings to reach him?"

Index

More Power Calling products and programs

We at Power Calling appreciate any ideas or cold calling experiences you have and would like to share. Write us a letter and be sure to include your name, address and telephone number.

We'll put you on our mailing list—you'll be the first to know about new products, special pricing and introductory offers on audio-cassette tapes, videos, and workbooks. We also offer workshops and seminars. Ask about our training courses—we will tailor a Power Calling program to fit your business. Call us (or send us a fax or postcard).

Joan Guiducci's
Power Calling
P.O. Box 2309
Mill Valley, CA 94942
TEL: 415/383-4780
FAX: 415/383-2759